EnterpriseOne Technical Developer Interview Questions, Answers and Explanations

By Terry Sanchez

EnterpriseOne Technical Developer Interview Questions, Answers and Explanations

ISBN 10: 1-933804-38-6

ISBN 13: 978-1-933804-38-5

Edited By: Jamie Fisher

The programs in this book have been included for instructional value only. They have been tested with care but are not guaranteed for any particular purpose. The publisher does not offer any warranties or representations nor does it accept any liabilities with respect to the programs.

Trademarks: All trademarks are the property of their respective owners. Equity Press is not associated with any product or vender mentioned in this book.

Please visit our website at www.oracookbook.com

Printed in the United States of America

Table of Contents

Question 1: Minimizing the size of .PDF

I want to suppress ".PDF" output (at least minimize the size of .PDF), when I create ".CSV" output from a UBE. If I mark the "Suppress All Output" on 'Report Properties', then ".CSV" will also be suppressed.

The bubble help on this check-box stated:

"If checked, a PDF file will not be produced for this report when run."

It didn't mention the ".CSV" output.

When I made the section invisible, or issue 'hide section' in 'do section' event, or issued 'suppress section' write in do 'section event', then an empty ".CSV" was generated.

The release time was: B9 - 8.93B1.

Is there a solution for this?

A: You can perform "Database Output" from the UBE to "text/CSV" file and suppress all output. This way, the "pdf" file will be suppressed but the text file will be generated.

Question 2: Command to use in ERW

I like to write some records into a temp table, and then by the end of execution clear the table.

Is there a command that I can use in ERW?

A: There are several ways to clear the file after processing.

In the last section of running UBE:
1. You can delete (using ER Code) on a key.
2. You can use the 'Call External Command' and "clrpfm", or use the OS's native way to clear a file from a command line.
3. You can also use a TC. If you delete with a TC, you can choose your data selection.

Another suggestion is, you can use "B8000002 Delete All Rows from Table" and retrieve, then free the environment handle calling "B8000007 BSFN" (before and after B8000002).

For added information, if your temporary table can be used by more concurrent processes (e.g. more are using the 'APPL/UBE' on different workstations and/or "citrix/wts" sessions), they can cause data collision.

To avoid this situation, you should begin all table indices with the same field, which is 'NextNumber', 'BatchNumber', and 'UniqueKeyID' type. Before all table operation, retrieve a 'NextNumber/NextID', which will be unique for your session. You can name it 'SessionID' and you can use it in all temporary table operation. After the job is done, you can delete your "session records" with a single key 'Delete Table I/O' using your 'SessionID' based on your primary key.

Question 3: Copying versions from R1 to R2

UBE R1 has 80 versions. OMW will only copy R1 template to R2.

Instead of creating 80 versions for R2 one by one, is there any way to copy all versions from R1 to R2?

A: You can try to copy the version table records (F983051, F98305V) and rename the 'UBE ID'.

Question 4: Conversion to Julian date

Can a date in the format of 26-DEC-05, can be converted into a Julian date?

A: If you can find a business function that takes the format mask as a parameter and calls the "DeformatDate api", then you should be able to use the mask: A-B-R (day-month abbreviation-year).

In your case, you may have to input 26-Dec-05 because the month abbreviation might not be accepted if it's all in capital letters.

Another suggestion is to convert date 'DD-MON-YYYY' to JDE date format using business function "Convert String Date to Date Format", i.e. 'B0800208' with a date mask of "MSDSR".

Question 5: Check-out error

I have an issue with tables in XE. When I do a checkout, change an index by adding or deleting a column, and then check it back in, everything looks fine. But if I checkout the object again, I received an error and the logging states "duplicate TAM spec".

What can I do about this?

A: You can try to delete the 6 spec file on the client machine.

Question 6: Triggers to Oracle under WEB client

I have a trouble with triggers in Oracle running under 'WEB' client. I created a new table (F554308L) to make a 'Log of Delegations' (F43008). This process is running perfectly under 'FAT', but if I use 'WEB', it didn't work.

The script is:

```
CREATE OR REPLACE TRIGGER
"CRPDTA"."F43008_BEFORE_DELETE" BEFORE DELETE ON
F43008 FOR EACH ROW
BEGIN
insert into crpdta.f554308L
(LADCTO,
LAARTG,
LADL01,
LAALIM,
LARPER,
LAATY,
LAEV01,
LAUPMJ,
LAUPMT,
LAJOBN,
LASECUSR,
LAAN8)
values
```

```
(:old.APDCTO,
ld.APARTG,
ld.APDL01,
ld.APALIM,
ld.APRPER,
ld.APATY,
'E',
TO_CHAR(SYSDATE, 'YYYYDDD')-1900000,
TO_CHAR(SYSDATE, 'HH24MISS'),
USERENV('TERMINAL'),
substr(USER,1,10),
ld.APRPER);
END F43008_Before_Delete;
ALTER TRIGGER "CRPDTA"."F43008_BEFORE_DELETE" ENABLE
```

The 'WEB' client didn't inform the oracle owner (like "testdta.delete" or "crpdta.delete") when I executed a transaction like delete, while the 'FAT' client did it. My ERP is 8.0 SP 22.

A: You can use the JDE table triggers. It would be better for operations like that.

Question 7: Multi-language setting

Is there an option to use multi-language in JDE like localization?

A: If you are referring to users using 'OW' with different language, you can set "Language Preference" in each user's profile. On the other hand, you must have and install the required language pack.

Both localization and language depends on user profile settings, in the order of 'Language' (LNGP) and 'Localization Country Code' (LCTR).

If the localization was developed and done well, then there should not be any collision between these settings. Some parts of the localization are not translated for all of your required language.

Question 8: Receipt Routing / F43092 / ACTO

I need to update the 'Active Operation' flagging the 'Receipt Routing' file (F43092). Is there a business function or another way to do it? I tried using "F43092EditLine BSFN", but I got confused with the number of versions and applications it asked for.

What other things will I need to do if I decide to update the 'ACTO' and Quantity, using Table I/O in ER? I'm doing this in a UBE.

A: The version that was asked for is the version of different applications. You can use "XJDE0001" version value to send to business function. There are writings about 'BSFN' that mimic the application "P43250". You can look into the 'Application P43250' row, exit 'Disposition/Movement' to see how this 'BSFN' works.

Question 9: HTML Report not submitting

I have a report that did not show up in submitted jobs when kicked off in html. The report runs fine in 'FAT' client local end server. I tried copying the report to a different name but got the same result.

What could be causing this?

A: The cause can't be determined but the solution is simple but painful, bounce your web server and it will start working.

Another suggestion is, if you are in 'AS400' and the report was revised, delete the "*SQL pkg". Also, when the 'jas' generation is done, make sure the 'Generate Report Licensing Information' is checked if doing individual report objects. You may or may not see this option; it depends on what SP you are on. There are cases where the problem is not resolved except by creating a new batch version on the web client, converting it, and going through the deploy process. This was the result of an update midstream in the development.

Question 10: the meaning of columns RPSFX and RPSFXE in F0411

What is the meaning and content of the columns 'RPSFX' and 'RPSFXE' in F0411 table?

A: In Xe:

RPSFX - Pay Item or line item, identifies each line of the AP voucher.

RPSFXE - Pay Item Extension Number identifies adjusting entries for each line item when it is not zero (i.e. when the Adjusting Document Type (RPDCTA) is not blank). For example, when an AP voucher is voided.

Question 11: jde.ini File for Visual Studio.net

I Installed 8.10 Demos in my PC, and then I Installed 'Visual Studio.net'. I was not able to open 'BSFN' through Business function design aid. I got the error "unable to open design tool msdev.exe".

Can you provide me with the correct 'jde.ini' settings?

A: You should have done the opposite. Install Visual studio before installing JDE. The JDE client picks the installation and refers it in the INI.

To fix your problem, do the following:

1. Open "JDE.INI".
2. Locate the "JDE_CG" section.
3. Replace "$COMP" with a folder location of your visual C installation, like "C:\Program Files\Microsoft VisualC\".

This can be executed in "ERP8.0".

Question 12: Bitmap in FDA 8.10

I am working with an application using 'FDA' and have added a new option in the menu/exit bar under row. This option is also checked to appear on the toolbar, which it does correctly. The problem is that the icon was not displayed on the toolbar. I have removed & added the bitmap "HC_FORM & HC_ROW" under the 'File option' and the 'Row option'. Neither has been successful in displaying the icon.

What can I do to display the icon?

I also thought that I should just create a custom bitmap for the application that I am working with. I know that I can add bitmaps to the 'res' folder.
Is there an option to create a bitmap?

A: If an existing "HC" type user overrides exist for the application, this user overrides are read and used when displaying the menu bar and toolbar options for the application. In order to see any new exits created within the design, locate any existing "HC" type user overrides for the application in the "User Overrides" application (P98950). Delete this user overrides. Then, when running the application, the new exit created will display.

Question 13: BOM (P30200) Issue on HTML

In the case of multi-level view while running the "BOM" application on HTML , if there are only 10 matching records in the table, those records come in the grid as 1-10 records with a down arrow. When I click that down arrow, I get those 10 records repeated again in the grid, i.e. 1-20 records get displayed and out of those 11-20, they are the same as the 1-10 records. I contacted Oracle and they said the change was in M1 tools release.

Is there any alternative to fix this?

A: It looks like the application is looping. It is using 'BSFN' to do the fetch from cache, but it doesn't know when to stop. You can verify if the "page at a time" is enabled, and if the data is fed into the grid using "Get custom grid row".

Question 14: Recommended settings and Encoding name in P98031

We are 4 weeks from going live on 8.11 SP1 and are having performance issues with our table conversion programs. We regularly run a large number of different conversions (inbound) over reasonably large files (1,000 to 50,000 records). One conversion in our current live environment (XE), takes 5-15 minutes. However, tests in 8.11 shows a typical run time of 2-3h.

One of the new requirements for TC in 8.11 is to setup an encoding name with cross reference in "P93081". I do not have any documentation as to what is the recommended setup. Our current settings are:

> User class: *PUBLIC
> Environment: *ALL
> Program ID: *DEFAULT
> Version: *DEFAULT
> Encoding Name: CP1252 (WIN-Latin 1, Western Europe)

Is this is the recommended setup?

Will performance improve if a different encoding name is used (e.g. UTF8)?

A: That is the most preferred settings. The other encoding type is not going to make a major difference to the processing time of the TC.

Question 15: Using SQL Stored Procedure within a UBE

I am trying to create a stored procedure that will sum up the data in our biggest transaction table, and then based on the user selections, return the data to a 'UBE'.I was not able to find any information on calling the "Oracle Stored Procedure" from a 'UBE'.

Is this possible? If it is, is there a code sample that I can look at?

A: I am not sure if this is possible. You can create a dummy table, and write a table triggers on backend. From there, you can call the stored proc to meet your need.
The following are the steps:

1. Create a dummy table.
2. Update/insert a record in this table. I would recommend an updated table and increment a value in that, e.g. 'UKID'.
3. Go to this dummy table in the backend, and write a trigger for an update. In this trigger, you can call your stored procedure.

For your perusal, I have done this in the past:

1. Create an SQL.
2. Embed within a batch file (have an attachment for reference).
3. Call a batch file through execute external program 'BSFN'.

```
   rpt_CmndLine [LGL1,String,50] =
"\\server\path\runsp.bat " Execute External
Program[CMFG,B34A1030,ExecuteExternalProgram]
   DS cSuppressErrorMessage [D34A1030,SUPPS] <- <Zero>
   DS cErrorCode [D34A1030,ERRC] ->
   DS szErrorMessageId [D34A1030,DTAI] ->
   DS szCommandLine [D34A1030,NFLF] <- rpt_CmndLine
```

You can also make the command line variable, and use it to fetch the values from a custom table based on Program ID.

Question 16: Prompting for Data Selection on menu

I'm currently designing a menu where there are a number of reports. I want the users to be prompted for the 'Data Selection' only when executing these reports. I'm able to either run it blindly (no PO or no data selection) and prompt for PO to be displayed only, or I can prompt for all the versions to be displayed. However, what I can't manage to do is to display only the 'Data selection' on execution. I know it can be done in World software, but I can't locate where this functionality is in OW.

All the reports have their own versions attached to them, and all PO are unique and should not be modified. However, there are times when the 'Data selection' needs to be altered, which is why I want only that part to be displayed when running the report.

Is there any alternative way for me to do this?

A: I am not sure of your version but this works on ERP8

On your menu design, when you are defining your report and options, you can select 'data selection' only and that would override the version settings.
Attach a snapshot, it might help. This applies to One World Explorer. If you are using 'Solution explorer', you can define it while adding a task.

Question 17: Previous Value of Grid Column

I tried to save the GC value on the grid "Row is entered" event to use during the 'Column Exit' and 'Change event'. That event did not fire as expected, and the GC value was from the previous row and not the one that was just entered.

I am using Oneworld/XE SP 22 and Microsoft SQL Server.
Is there an easy way to determine what the previous value was during a 'Column Exit' and 'Change event' on a grid?

A: You can fix it with the following steps:

1) Create a new column in the grid for each value that you need from the previous value.
2) When the grid fills up initially, add the code "Grid Record is fetched" event to set the GC value for the new previous column to current BC value. You can also use the "Write Grid Line - After" event.
3) At the end of the "Row is exited and changed" event, add the code to set the new previous column to the current value. Whenever the value changes, the new "previous" column will always have the previous value.

It's better to add a grid scope variable for the previous value instead of GC Grid Columns. The following are the reasons for it:

1.) GC columns requires extra processing (e.g. Event, Validation, Formatting, etc.), while grid variables do not.
2.) Changing GC values in the 'Row Exited' and 'Changed XXX' events can sometimes randomly trigger 'YYY Exited' and 'Changed XXX' events again, depending on the cursor movement of the user.

Question 18: Changing a unique key on a production file

I created a custom table that is keyed like the "F4211". It holds additional information that is associated to the 'sales order detail file'. It was a 1:1 requirement.

Recently, my users need to attach many (unique) records to the custom file.
This file holds a return air bill number (for RMA) for that line. The old rule was 1 line to 1 part, now it is 1 line to 500 parts. If I include the air bill number as a key field, it would meet that requirement. I have to rebuild the maintenance from a 'Fix Inspect' to either a 'Header' or 'Header less' detail form.

Is JDE going to throw up if I change this 'unique key' and make it more unique?

A: If you need multiple "F4211" records to be unique in your custom table, use the 'LNID', or else make 'Suffix' or change orders 001, 002 etc. You can add a 'UKID' to your custom table then export the data, re-import the data with UKID, and change your table inserts to use a 'UKID' in your custom table. You will be able to have as many records unique as you like.
It's better not to change the primary keys. If you do, you have to deal with the following issues:

1) Backup the data and recreate with the 'Unique key'.
2) Specs issue in the server.

Another suggestion is to create a new table with the new additional data. It would be much cleaner, and would have no impact on current table, views, and apps.

If you still want to do it and add it to the existing table, and your database is on the AS400, you will need to clear all SQL packages before the new key is recognized.

Question 19: NER from DTS Package

We are implementing a document imaging solution that involves connecting to SQL Server 2000 for the staging tables. The 'Doc Imaging Vendor' has Java API's. I can't find a way to call those API's. We went to the staging table in SQL Server for a solution.

I want to call the 'NER Wrapper' to do voucher process from the 'DTS Package' attached to the staging table as a trigger.

Is there a better approach for this?

How can I execute the 'NER' from DTS Package?

A: You can get the document on "COM Interoperability" from PSFT site.
It will explain how to create a COM wrapper for "JDE", "BSFN", and "NER".

Question 20: 3 Way Match

How can I automate a three way match? I'm going to document an imaging solution for invoicing, and I do not want to use evaluated receipts (R43800) unnecessarily.

A: You could use the EDI tables which do not necessarily bring in the data using EDI. You could populate "F47031, 32 and 34". Although there are some fields which are required to be populated, even if the field name is different. In the 'ref. field', you need to populate the address number. But in 'KG', you must get documentation for this.

The EDI Files are "F47041", "F47042" and "F47044". These files could be leveraged to do the 3 Way Match to create the voucher.

Question 21: Insert blank row after level break on tabular report

I have a tabular financial report that is sequenced by object account and subtotals by 'LOD'.

Is there any business function or insert that I can use in my event rules, to tell the report to insert a blank line after each LOD break?

A: You can do the following steps but it's still untested:

1. Write a group section, make it conditional.
2. Enter 'constant' on report and put some blanks as value.
3. Call this section in level break section.

Question 22: Processing Options screen and UBE

I have a processing options screen that gives the users the choice of 12 options (only one can be filled in at runtime). Is there a way to determine which option was selected without writing a lot of "If statements"? I.e. If Option 1 is not equal to NULL, or Option 1 is not equal to blank, use variable.

How can I pick up a single option that has a value in it?

A: You should consider having just one processing option (perhaps a numeric-type field), and list the different values in the processing option description. Then, the user would just enter the appropriate value.

Here's a sample:

Processing Option 1
- 1 = Daily
- 2 = Weekly

- 3 = Monthly
- 4 = Quarterly (and so on)

Another suggestion is, to know the PO number that was selected. I.e. Suppose PO Option3 was selected; you need to get number 3.

Define 12 PO's of numeric size 2. In the version, pre-define each PO value in increasing value of 1. That is, PO Option 1 will have a value of 1. PO Option 2 will have a value of 2, and so on until PO option 12 will have a value of 12.

The user, instead of selecting a PO by putting a value, has to clear the contents of the PO which he wants to select. I.e. suppose Option 5 is to be selected, he will blank out the value within PO option 5.

Now in ER, add up all the PO values into a variable in a single mathematical expression:

```
        VA evt_SumofPOs = PO Option1 + PO Option2
+.....PO Option12
```

Next, subtract the total from 78, and then you will have the PO number that was selected.

```
        VA evt_POSelected = 78 - VA evt_SumofPOs
```

Supposing Option 5 was selected, (i.e blanked out by the user) then VA "evt_SumofPO's" will be 5 short (i.e. 73).

Hence, 78 - 73 = 5, the option was selected.

There is another option; you can consider using a 'Form' instead of a 'Processing Option Template'. If you use a 'Form' to submit the UBE, you can force only one
valid entry at a time and you can alert runtime that more than one option is being used.

Question 23: Jobs at SND status on AS400

When I submit a job from OW, the job was completed. But when I print it from the "submitted jobs", it did not print.

I saw the job at "SND" status on the "AS400 OUTQ". I was able to print if I open the "PDF" and print, but direct printing from "JDE" doesn't seem to work.

How can I handle this problem?

A: If the job stays in the "SND" status, then your "OUTQ" for this printer is not configured correctly for the printer you are using. The reason might be the 'IP' address was incorrect, or the 'Host Print Transform' option needed to be turned on, and choose the proper 'Manufacturer' and 'Model'. You can use the "*HP4" option. But if you have some 'funny' type of printer, this might not work.

Here is a sample setup:

```
Status:
Writer active . . . . . . . . . . . : Y
Writer name (s) if active . . . . . . : ACCOUNTS2
Output queue held . . . . . . . . . : N
Maximum spooled file size:
Number of pages . . . . . . . . . . : *NONE
Starting time . . . . . . . . . . . :
Ending time . . . . . . . . . . . . :
Writers to autostart . . . . . . . . : 1
Display any file . . . . . . . . . . : *NO
Job separators . . . . . . . . . . . : 0
Operator controlled . . . . . . . . : *YES
Order of files on queue . . . . . . . : *FIFO
Data queue . . . . . . . . . . . . . : *NONE
Library . . . . . . . . . . . . . . :

Authority to check . . . . . . . . . : *OWNER


Remote system . . . . . . . . . . . : *INTNETADR
```

```
Remote printer queue . . . . . . . . : *NONE


Queue for writer messages . . . . . . : QSYSOPR
Library . . . . . . . . . . . . . . : *LIBL
Connection type . . . . . . . . . . : *IP
Internet address . . . . . . . . . . : 10.1.1.55
Destination type . . . . . . . . . . : *OTHER
Host print transform . . . . . . . . : *YES
Manufacturer type and model . . . . . : *RICOH2035
Workstation customizing object . . . . : LEXFORM
Library . . . . . . . . . . . . . . : QGPL
Image configuration . . . . . . . . : *NONE
Destination options . . . . . . . . : *NONE


Print separator page . . . . . . . . : *NO
User defined option . . . . . . . . : *NONE
User defined object:
Object . . . . . . . . . . . . . . : *NONE
Library . . . . . . . . . . . . . . :
Object type . . . . . . . . . . . . :
User driver program . . . . . . . . : *NONE
Library . . . . . . . . . . . . . . :
Spooled file ASP . . . . . . . . . . : *SYSTEM
Text description . . . . . . . . . . : Accounts
Printer Optra
```

Return-path: Received: from mail.hunterdouglas.com.au
(mailmarshal.hunterdouglas.com.au [10.2.2.6]) by
mail.hunterdouglas.com.au; Tue, 28 Mar 2006 13:16:55
+1100 Received:
from srvr01.host53.com (Not Verified[216.127.80.127])
by
mail.hunterdouglas.com.au with ESMTP Generic id ;
Tue, 28 Mar 2006
12:15:05 +1000 X-ClientAddr: 127.0.0.1 Received: from
srvr01.host53.com

(localhost.localdomain [127.0.0.1]) by
srvr01.host53.com
(8.12.11/8.12.11) with ESMTP id k2S2IQcW031294; Mon,
27 Mar 2006
20:18:26 -0600 Received: (from apache@localhost) by
srvr01.host53.com
(8.12.11/8.12.11/Submit) id k2S2IQEg031290; Mon, 27
Mar 2006 20:18:26

-0600 Date: Mon, 27 Mar 2006 20:18:26 -0600 Message-Id: jdelistsubscribers@jdelist.com From: JFreak Reply-to: JD Edwards® EnterpriseOne Developers Errors-to: jdeowdev-bounces@jdelist.com Sender: jdeowdev-bounces@jdelist.com MIME-Version: 1.0 Content-type: text/html; charset=iso-8859-1 Subject: Re: Jobs at SND status on AS400 X-jdelist.com-MailScanner-Information: Please contact the ISP for more information X-jdelist.com-MailScanner: Found to be clean Cont ent-Transfer-Encoding: quoted-printable X-MIME-Autoconverted: from 8bit to quoted-printable by srvr01.host53.com id k2S2IQcW031294

Question 24: Comparing Account Balances to Transactions

I have been in contact with response line, and have copies of the ER for the UBE from 8.10. The ER calls a new 'BSFN', which I have a copy of, but I was not able to get it built on the system. Response line indicates development will not create a one-off for ERP8.0. The report is set to compare the files for fiscal year 2006, and still takes about 7 hours to complete on the weekend (no users on the system), and will only get worse as the year goes on.

These are the specs that we are using: ERP8.0, IBM iSeries, and Citrix thin-client for functional users.

How can I speed up "R09705" in "ERP8.0"?

A: There are two versions for this report, one for the balance sheet accounts and one for the income statement accounts. You can run it on the 'AA' ledger. Both reports run concurrently every night in the scheduled batches and usually were completed in about an hour. When it was run as a single report, it would usually be terminated by the scheduler after two hours.

You can use a data selection. You are right that restricting processing of some reports with data selection can produce unpredictable results. However, think about what you can do with this report, you can simply confirm all the transactions in the ledger which are included in the monthly summaries. You can sum up transactions by year, month, and account number in the 'Account Ledger table' (F0911), and compare them to the same year, month, and account number in the 'Account Balances table' (F0902). It's not writing any records.

Similarly, you can also develop customized version for 'Account Balances' to 'Ledger' which runs on every weekend, separately for 'Income Statement and Balance' sheet accounts. In fact, you can have that option to open in your 'Processing option "Select"

Tab', because before running customized version you can use the same 'Tab' wherein you can give 'Beginning Object Account' and 'Ending Object Account'. You can use that in 8.11.

Question 25: Partial Line Shipments Allowed

There is a field in "F4211" files (SDAPTS), that indicates if the line is allowed for partial shipments or not. This information is from customer master, but our users want to modify it when they create or update a sales order. I checked the 'BSFN' (S421002C Sales Order Line View Controller) that it used for the saved information, but there wasn't a way to update this field.

Do you have any idea how I can do that?

Where can I find information about how the 'BSFN' works to create or update sales orders?

The modification must be in the app. "P421002". This is a sub-form that is inside of the form "P42101/W42101D". The problem is that there wasn't any view associated, and all the information was managed by 'BSFN', but this field was not included in it. This 'BSFN' saved the information in a cache that I don't know where, and after that other 'BSFN' saved the information in the "F4211". I tried to follow all the processing, but failed.

If I modify this field, the rest of the process must be in the standard of JDE because the shipping programs work with this field properly. I tried to modify it by SQL and followed the normal shipping process, all worked properly.

A: You can't update the "F4211.SDAPTS" field without changing the 'Business Function B4200311'.

A look in this function tells me that the 'APTS' value was retrieved from the Customer Master by a call to the business function "MBFCustomerMaster" 'N0100042' and stored in the 'F42UI01' cache.

Adding a field in the application will not help. You'll have to make changes in the 'B4200311' to override the field value.

Another suggestion is if you are not worried about making modifications, you can look into what it would take to add the data item to the business view and modify the form, and business function. It is really frustrating when the data item you want is not in the business view.

An example is, you can make a copy of the 'APPL', and Business View, and then go and make modifications and preserving the vanilla. A lot of companies want to stay vanilla, but you can't let the software guide your business and 'SOE' is one of the 'APPL' that seems to need the most modifications.
You should take not that you do not have to modify too many business functions. Only the "B4200311" (The "Grandmother" of all Sales Order Functions) needs to be changed at the point where it retrieves the 'Customer Master' record, using the call to "MBFCustomerMaster" 'N0100042'.

After the record is retrieved, you'll have to add custom code to replace the partial shipments allowed field (cPartialShipmntsAllowY) with a 'Y' and then let JDE code to do the rest.

You should also take note that making mod to 'Sales Order Entry' is bad in XE, but it's nothing compared to 8.11 (if you're using the Power Forms P42101).

The final resolution to this is not really a "good" programming, but it will probably accomplish what you need and in a lesser time. In 'P421002', add the grid column for your 'Partial Shipments Allowed'. When a user changes the value, write it to a work file (you'll need to create it), keyed by the "SessionKey", "Order Number", "Order Type", "Order Company", and "Line Number". Then, put one more mod in 'P42101' on the OK button (Post Button Clicked "Asynch"). After all the 'F4211' records are written, read your work file and do an update to 'F4211' to set the 'Partial Ship Allowed' the way your users want it. This should work if your SQL updates were doing the trick.

Question 26: Error in Table Conversion (CSV to Oneworld table)

I got this error while doing table conversion:

```
        Opening UBE Log for report R55TEST2, version
AML0001
        --UBE--[0]-- Start Time : 10:12:36
        TCEngine Level 0
\b9\system\TCEngine\tcdtaref.c: TCE009025
        - Could not find column sequence 72
        --UBE--[0]-- End Time : 10:12:52
        UBE Job Finished with Error(s).
```
Increase Debug Level into your jde.ini to view the cause of this error.

What should I do?

A: There are a few things you should check in order to make it correct:

1. Check whether your "csv" file column sequence, and oneworld table column sequence is the same.
2. Check if your mapping is proper or not.
3. Check your data type and length of data items.

Question 27: Different types of action in XMLRequest inbound transaction

I tried to get all the parameters for inbound transaction using XML interoperability.

In interoperability document, there was only one example which returned the information about outbound transaction:

```
<?xml version='1.0' ?>
<jdeRequest type='trans' user='user'
pwd='password'
environment='environment' session='
` sessionidle='300'>
<transaction action='transactionInfo'
type='JDESOOUT'>
</transaction>
</jdeRequest>
```

When this request was sent to 'ENT' server, the response contained all fields and parameters for outbound transaction "JDESOOUT".

I need similar information for inbound transaction.

When I tried the same request with inbound transaction "JDEPOIN", it gave the error:

```
<?xml version='1.0' encoding='UTF-8' ?>
<jdeResponse role='*ALL' type='trans'
user='PSFT' xmlns='urn:Schemas-
    jdedwards-com:trans.response.JDEPOIN'
session='2652.1143108236.16'
    environment='PD810'>
<transaction type='JDEPOIN'
action='transactionInfo'>
<returnCode code='20'>ERROR</returnCode>
<ERROR>No entry found in cross reference
table for outbound transaction
    Type: JDEPOIN</ERROR>
</transaction>
</jdeResponse>
```

How can I get all the parameters and fields for inbound transaction using xml interoperability?

Is it possible to get required batch system use for inbound transaction using control tables? I need this information at runtime only.

A: Try to run "P47002". You will see there how transactions are defined. You can even define your own transactions. You can define into what table header the record goes and into where the detail goes. In XML messages, you refer to column names of mentioned tables.

The only catch is that tables must have certain fields. Otherwise, XML transaction processor fails to work. Those are: "EDUS", "EDBT", "EDTN", "EDLN".

Question 28: PDF guide on JDE APIs - XE

I lost my PDF document guide on "JDE API (XE)" for "C BSFN". I need the C language "JDE API's" (XE only, bc B8.9 are starting to have different API's with Unicode).

Where can I get it? I could not find it on KG anymore.

A: Very few API's are actually documented. The ones that were documented have sparse documentation, outdated documentation, or are just plain wrong. Some of the API calls within a group of calls that may be listed, others are not.

For you to do a 'JDE C' development you can get a good text editor or utility that can search for text in files (one suggestion is the "Ultra Edit").

You can search all the "*.h files in ...systeminclude\" for key words, phrases or known function calls, and then look at some of the other API calls that are there. Search all of the "*.c files in ...[Dev Env]\" source for those API calls, and reverse engineer how the JDE programmers use them. This often leads to more API calls which leads to searching the "*.h" files again. You can use frequently the search capabilities of the text editor to look up enumerations.

Question 29: E811 External Program

How can I run an external program from E811 web page?

In my case, I need to run the Excel for opening a specific pivot table (.xls) that is available in the user workstation.

A: You can try the following:

```
0005 //
0006 Execute External Program
"1" -> cSuppressErrorMessage
BF szCopyToExtract -> szCommandLine
0007 //
0008 //
0009 // CPYTOSTMF
FROMMBR('/qsys.lib/outbound.lib/jdeextract.file/Table
Name.mbr')
0010 // TOSTMF('BF ISFLocation') STMFOPT(*REPLACE)
DBFCCSID(37)
0011 // STMFCODPAG(*PCASCII)          ·
0012 //
0013 BF szCopyToIFS = CPYTOSTMF
FROMMBR('/qsys.lib/outbound.lib/jdeextract.file/Table
Name.mbr')
TOSTMF('BF ISFLocation') STMFOPT(*REPLACE)
DBFCCSID(37) STMFCODPAG(*PCASCII)
0014 //
0015 Execute External Program
"1" -> cSuppressErrorMessage
BF szCopyToIFS -> szCommandLine
0016 //
0017 //
0018 // CHGAUT
OBJ('/DIXIEDATA/Extracts/ScriptFile.txt')
USER(*PUBLIC) DTAAUT(*RWX)
0019 // OBJAUT(*SAME)
0020 //
0021 BF szChangeAuthority = CHGAUT
OBJ('/DIXIEDATA/Extracts/ScriptFile.txt')
USER(*PUBLIC) DTAAUT(*RWX)OBJAUT(*SAME)

0022 //
0023 Execute External Program
"1" -> cSuppressErrorMessage
BF szChangeAuthority -> szCommandLine
```

Question 30: Applying a small ESU on a workstation

I have a small ESU to apply. It only has 3 SAR in it and affects two objects.

Can this be applied on a local work station? Should it be built on a deployment server?

A: You will need to build the package on your deployment server first, then deploy to that workstation only. However, if the object that you are testing is set to run on the enterprise server, you will need to override the object and to run the workstation on "*LOCAL".
This way if the ESU does not work, it is much easier and cleaner to back the ESU out.

Question 31: Force "Row Exit and Change" Process

I tried to force a 'Row Exit and Changed' process in an application without user input. I have a custom "Submit" row exit button on "P4310". It works with 'Order Headers' which should call the 'Order detail' screen (W4310), and also process all the logic in the "Row Exit and Changed" event without the user input before the user clicks "OK".

What should be the follow-up?

A: When "OK" is pressed, "Row Exit and changed" (REAC) event is called automatically. It is not necessary for the user to change from that row or press enter, or anything. "OK" does process REAC event.

But, if you must, then you need to put a push button on the form and put all the logic in there. Then hide the button, and press it from your row exit event.

You can press the "OK" button with the system function call from the 'Post Dialog is initialized'.

Set a flag for "OK" button to know that it was pressed programmatically, so it can issue a 'dummy error' to prevent it to exit the form, and skip the normal event rule execution. You can clear this 'dummy error' after pressing the "OK" in the 'Post Dialog is initialized'.

What is missing is the actual trigger to make the toolset believe that something on the grid has changed, and that the line needs to pass through row is exited async.

These are the steps you can do:
1). Add a new hidden trigger field to the grid.
2). Write grid line afterwards, and populate the new grid field.
3). In the last grid record written, set a flag to force error in "OK" button, press 'ok', then clear the error. Set off the flag.
4). In "OK" button, if flag force error is on, issue error and then exit "OK" button.

Question 32: Field in data selection user input

Is there a way to ignore one of the data selections that the user input? I can't control the user from key in the data selection. Can I control and ignore the data selection user input?

For example, I want to ignore only the data selection keyed in by the user (e.g. the date field, but other fields are ok). Whether the user key in or not key in the date field, in the event rule, I will overwrite the date field input by the user.

Is it workable?

A: Under 'System Functions' select 'Set Selection Append Flag' and set it to 'No'. This will cause the application to ignore any selections set by the user. Then use processing options to allow the user to enter only the values you want to allow them to select with. Use 'ER' to build the data selection from the processing options.

I assume that you require the field in your business view. You could create a copy of the business view that does not include any fields that you do not want to allow the data selection on. Use this new business view in a driver section, and then use the system function 'Use data sel/seq from a section' in the original driver section. This way the user never sees the fields that you do not want them to put the data selection on. This was tested in 8.11, and it does not seem to matter that the business views are not identical.

Question 33: Insert Text in TXFT field of Foo165 (8.11)

I'm using Table Conversion tool in E1 8.11 to convert legacy data in AS400 to E1 DB which is on IBM DB/2. The client has a table in AS400 which holds the Item master specifications. They want this data to be attached as Item master attachments.

Using Table conversion, I can link and insert all fields, except inserting record into "GDTXFT" field of "Foo165" table. Is there a standard BSFN to insert text values into "GDTXFT"? If there is, which one is it?

A: You can use the "ConvertNarrativeText" BSFN. This BSFN converts the text passed as parameter to the binary field and writes the row in the "Foo165" table. This last point means that you have to disable the 'write' in your TC.

The problem with this BSFN is that it is developed to insert information attached to the additional database, so it's expected that the first parameter is "GT00092" (media object for additional database) and not "GT4101" (the one we have to use).

With this information, we can call to the BSFN with the following parameters:

```
        Write World Narrative Text to One World
Generic Text (F00165
        "GT00092" -> szOBNM
        "X" -> szTypeofData
        Short item Number -> mnSuppDataNumericKey1
        "Text" -> szGenericTextItemName
        Attachment text -> szMO_Text_Blob
```

This will write a row in the "Foo165" table, but not a good one, because you have in the "GDOBNM" field the value "GT00092", and in the "GDTXKY" (with short item number = 72228) like '|X|||72228|0||'. You can see that this string have the value of "szTypeofData" parameter concatenated with the short item number and some '|'.

So, after you run the BSFN, you can make and update to the "Foo0165", changing the value of "GDOBNM" to "GT4101" and "GDTXKY" to "72228" (the item number).

Question 34: Positive Pay Sleep Mode

I was planning to implement 'Positive Pay' interface on JDE 8.0 SQL 2K. I have reached a point wherein I created the text file on the network location that needs to be sent to bank. As of now, the user has to manually log-on to the bank website, and then do the file selection and send.

Is there anything that I can do to easily send this file to the bank without the user intervention? Can this be done as soon as the file is created on the network location at the end of the day?

A: There is an application that a bank can produce to make things easier, and still secure to send the files. It still requires a log-on and codes for sending the file. There are created interfaces for this application. I would suggest that you talk to your bank about ways to transfer the files and improve it.

Question 35: Debug Settings

These are the JDE.INI settings:

When I run 'UBE' on the server, I take 'row exit' and set to "UBE Logging Level = 6".

I got the following log:

```
Mar 17 11:28:47 ** 2636/1624 ODBC:S DBResetRequest
conn=01D03BD8 hd=049D2F08 dr=04999C88 JDEDEV01 A
(JDE@Business Data - CRP)
Mar 17 11:28:47 ** 2636/1624 SELECT * FROM
CRPDTA.F44H71W1 WHERE ( GWGENJOB = 10672.000000 AND
GWMCU = ' 430230042' AND GWOBJ = '15280 ' AND GWSUB =
'42370 ' AND GWOPTION = ' ' AND GWOPKID = ' ' ) ORDER
BY GWGENJOB ASC,GWMCU ASC,GWOBJ ASC,GWSUB
ASC,GWOPTION ASC,GWAN8 ASC,GWITM ASC,GWSEQ ASC
--UBE--[4]-- --ER: Line(45): Done Processing File
I/O.
--UBE--[4]-- --ER: Line(46): <Processing File I/O>
F44H71W1
--UBE--[4]-- --ER:: Fetch Next....
Mar 17 11:28:47 ** 2636/1624 Entering JDB_Fetch
Mar 17 11:28:47 ** 2636/1624 Entering
JDB_ClearSelection
Mar 17 11:28:47 ** 2636/1624 Entering
JDB_ClearSequencing
--UBE--[4]-- --ER: Line(46): Done Processing File
I/O.
--UBE--[4]-- --ER: Line(51): <Processing IF/WHILE> If
SV File_IO_Status is not equal to CO SUCCESS
--UBE--[4]-- --ER: Line(51): <Condition in IF/WHILE
met> If SV File_IO_Status is not equal to CO SUCCESS
--UBE--[4]-- --ER: Line(52): <Processing Assign> VA
evt_cExitLoop_EV01 = "1"
--UBE--[4]-- --ER: Line(52): Done Processing Assign
--UBE--[4]-- --ER: Line(53): <Processing
ENDIF/ENDWHILE> End If
--UBE--[4]-- --ER: Line(53): <Done Processing
ENDIF/ENDWHILE>
```

When I run it locally, how can I get the same result?
I tried under 'DEBUG' in 'INI' as "UBEDebuglevel = 6". It showed a regular log which was different from the one stated.

What is the solution?

A: In [DEBUG] section, "Output=FILE" should do it.

```
    Xe - SP 20 UD 6 / ES NT - W2K - SQL 2K / Clients
- XP Pro
    E8.0 - SP 20 / ES NT - W2K - SQL 2K / Clients -
XP Pro
    E8.9 - SP 2 / ES NT - W2k - SQL 2K / Clients -
XP Pro
```

While running the UBE, select the 'Advanced Option'. It's in the 'row exit' button. It is available while running. Here, you can actually choose to tick the debugging level and have all the logging options on in this screen. Set the log level from the 'Visual' assist to 6. Then, run the report locally. Once done, you can get the log in the 'Print queue folder'.

Question 36: Binding service programs on the iSeries

I want to implement "Enterprise One" (version 8.95 with the 8.11 tools set) and try to bind BSFN to RPG service programs. I was not able to find the right 'jde.ini' parameters to make this work.

I got the following error in the 'job log':

```
        30 03/15/06 08:22:02.094352 QCANPARS QSYS 0625
JDELIB
        To module . . . . . . . . . : JDE400U
        To procedure . . . . . . . : ExecuteCmd
        Statement . . . . . . . . . : 13
        Message . . . . : Qualifier missing from
qualified
        name 'THCGPRDDV '.
        Cause . . . . . : A qualifier delimiter
character was
        specified, but no qualifier was found.
        Recovery . . . : Specify the missing qualifier
or
        specify *N if no value is required for the
qualifier.
```

I need to use this functionality to connect to legacy code, which needs to be called in a highly efficient manner.

What can be the solution for this?

A: The error is coming from the IBM command analyzer 'QCA'. This is the program that validates command parameters, and calls command processing programs. Some command parameter is being passed as blank but the underlying command wants a value. The blank value is part of a qualified name as in "lib/file". It would be helpful to know what command generated this message, and figure out which parameter value are missing then work backwards to the solution. It could be an IBM command or a JDE created command. The error suggests a missing name in a qualified name which could be a library, service program, table, or a "*LIBL" command parameter. Contemplate the business function creation parameters in the 'INI' file.

You can also check if you turned on the "Use Owner" on the data source. That inserts a dot in front of table names, and then when sending SQL to the server, inserts the database table owner. If the owner name in the data source is blank, you get ".name". The leading dot might be telling the command analyzer that this is part of a qualified name, and triggers that error message. 'Dot' was the qualified name separator in an ancient version of the 'iSeries' product, the genes to respond to a leading, or a trailing dot may still exist in the command analyzer code.

There is another suggested solution for your problem. Troubleshooting such problems is easier if you have the command that failed. If you have it, you can try to copy or paste it to a green screen command line and see what happens. You might need to set up such things as the correct library list to allow the command to execute correctly.

Question 37: Event rule not executing in Debugger only

I added some code to the 'Line is Exited and Changed (Asynchronous) Event' in the grid of the "P1721". At first, I thought that the data selection was too tight but after removing the 'data selection', I found out that the event rule 'PS Button' (refers to a button on the Exit bar [cop Selected row]) was not executed.

It only worked when I used the debugger, deleted the line, and added it again. There was no result. I tried to rename the button but it only works in debugger.

What could be the reason for this?

A: When you run the debugger, it runs events in 'Sync' mode. You will need to move that event to the 'Inline' event.

Try to search the "Knowledge Garden" for this string "Press Button and debug". You will find some items that will explain what's going on. The bad news is that the problem seems to go back to the windows level, and JDE does not take further action on it. You can overcome the problem by inserting a (dummy) 'Form Interconnect' right before the 'Press Button' event rule.

Question 38: Retrieve server job number

Is it possible to get the server job number of a UBE during runtime?

A: If there is no BSFN which returns the 'Job Number', you can do a fetch on the "F986110" table.

This is the table which contains the 'JOB' details for any job running on the server.

Question 39: Purchase Orders

I am new to using the 'PO Module'. When a 'PO' is entered and a change was made on the same day, the complete 'PO' will print. When I add an item several days later, the PO will only print the added item. I thought it might have something to do with the status codes we are using in the PO sub-system.

What can I do to have a complete print of the 'PO"?

A: It is involved with the 'Status Codes' and 'Activity Rules' you have setup. When you are using the 'Auto Print Subsystem', the version it runs to "print" the 'PO' has the proc. opt to update the status code set, so the 'activity rules' move those status forward to a status representing that the line has printed. Then, when you add new lines, the 'auto print subsystem' picks up the new lines because their status indicates these lines were not printed while the other was printed. If you want all the lines of the 'PO', you will need to setup a 'reprint version' of "P43500" that has the proc. opt set to "not advance". The status is forward, and also checks the status codes that are allowed to print. You can also include in the 'reprint version' (in the Data Selections) to not print any lines with a 'Last Status of 980', which are cancelled lines.

Question 40: Showcase

I need to be able to allow the operator to select a date using the "MMDDYY" format. Showcase treats this field as just a numeric field. This field (DLIJ) is in 'JDE DD', and the file "F0301" is in the SVR.

How can I indicate to "Showcase" that a field is stored as a Julian Date in JDE?

How can I display it in a "MM/DD/YY" format?

A: Once you defined your "date_field" as "DATE (date_field, CYYDDD)", the condition should be applied on that expression, not into the field itself.

Also, your prompt values should be typed as "MM/DD/YYYY" (e.g. "11/10/2005").

When you first installed showcase, there was an option to say whether you were running JDE software, you should have selected this. This ties the JDE Software Repository (SVR), Data dictionary, and security to JDE tables. You should also check the installation codeThe user profile signing into showcase must also have "JDFOBJ" in the library list, and one of the "JDEINIT*" programs as the 'called' program.

If the data you are speaking of is a custom table and not a JDE table, then add the table to the Software Repository (SVR). This will create the link so that the fields are defined correctly.

Question 41: Order Advance Pricing

I'm in the process of changing from 'JDE World' to 'SAP', and have just converted 2 of my 4 locations. This means that I can't use "ST" or "OT" transfer orders to transfer between plants. I'm using regular Sales Orders.

I'm using this for 'Raw Materials' also, which does not have 'Base Prices', but only 'Costs'. The 'Sales Price' is currently coming up as zero for 'Raw Materials'. There are hundreds of items, and the 'Cost Price' changes. The "sold to address" is my plant address, only 3 of those are used. The alternative thing to do is to modify "P4211", which I don't prefer to do.

Is there an easy way to force this to equal the 'Cost Price', without having to define a 'Base Price' for all of the raw materials?

A: You can use 'Advanced Pricing'. Just setup an adjustment for the 'sold to address' where the BC (Basis Code) is 3. It is similar in World.

Double check if your adjustment has an entry for the same unit of measure, as the pricing unit of measure to your item. Make sure that the adjustment schedule is attached to the customer master of the "Branch Plants".

Question 42: Search Type Security

Can you explain how Search Type Security works?

I can't figure out how to use it. From the 'G94' menu, I turned it on, but it didn't indicated how to setup different users with different search types. From what I saw, it's basically on or off, but I don't know what turning it on does.

Can you give me some information about it?

A: Search Type security restricts viewing 'Address Book' records by 'Search Type' in the 'Name Search' and 'Address Book Information' programs. Each 'Search Type' is defined as a separate table within system "code 94".

To set up 'Name Search Type' security:

From General Systems (G00), choose General User Defined Codes.

1. Enter a user ID in the 'Character Code' field to grant authority to that 'Search Type'. Each individual typed here have authority to customers only. Individuals not added for any Search Type doesn't have authority.

2. Press 'F5' to view the 'User Defined Code Types' form, which will show you all the available 'Search Types'.

3. Enter 'Search Type' codes that you have defined as valid values. A 'Code Type = @' grants authority to search all.

4. From 'Security Officer' (G94), choose 'Name Search Type'.

5. Enter 'Y' or 'N' in the 'Search Type Security' field. If set to 'Y', you must set up 'User Defined Codes' to grant authority.

This security only works for programs "P01051" and "P01200". Reporting is not affected by 'Name Search Type Security'. A group profile is not valid.

You need to use system 'code 94', and there is a 'UDC' set up for each standard search type. In the manual, you can deduce this by looking at the screenshot, but it does not state this implicitly. Then, you need to use the code type.

For example, if you want to grant someone an access to "S/T C (customers)" only, you would enter in the UDC video (V00051) System "Code 94". 'User Defined Codes C', and then under the 'Code' column enter the 'User ID'. Then, 'Add' or 'Change'. Now, this user will have access to 'ST=C' only.

You should remember to define all the search type setups in "G00 #14" first, by UDC code, and then turn on the "switch" in the "G94 #6" option. If you mark it as "Y" and no one is defined, you'll lock them all out of that environment for all search types in the address book. This search type security only affects "P01051" and "P01200".

Question 43: Counting user license

I have a problem with counting user license. When the user opens two sessions on the same machine and profiles to logon, the manager should count them as one license. That is with one exception. Sometimes, when the users uses two sessions, the manager "takes" two licenses. It only happens for one user "in time" (but not always the same user). After a few hours, one additional license is "free" again, and two sessions take one license. The next day, this problem is connected with the other user.

What could be the reason for this?

A: You can reset the license manager stuff. To do so, everyone needs to be out of the system.

First, find and delete the files "JDE_IDX_1" (thru 6), and they should be in "QGPL'. Assuming you are using "QSECOFR" profile (or something similar), "ADDLIBLE JDFOBJ" (or whatever your library is), submit a job calling "J98802JQ". This rebuilds the files you deleted. Check to make sure they all exist after this job is done.

There is a white paper on the 'Knowledge Garden' regarding this whole process.

Question 44: Mobile access

I need to provide "mobile" access to JDE. Some of our "service men" travels and they need to input or retrieve some data to or from JDE in every place.

There are two (hardware) solutions presented:
1) To use notebooks.
2) To use mobile devices (palm top, laptop, etc.)

And three software solutions:
a) VPN and Client Access.
b) Web browser and "web enabled JDE".
c) Create dedicated software for JDE access.

The easiest solution is VPN and Client Access, some cheap laptop, but cheap laptop also means not so "durable" plastic body. Cool laptops, like IBM (I mean 25 laptops) is quite big cost. A laptop is easy to manage, but is also easy to "receive" a virus.

The two hardware solutions are considered. While the first software solution is not available, the second one is possible but currently, my JDE is not "web enabled". The third software solution is probably the "most safe" solution but also expensive.

What is the best solution?

A: You could also consider a laptop with 'Remote Desktop' functionality. This still need a 'VPN' or similar connection, but it could use a local machine for the client access. It only needs a copy of windows professional on the laptop and you could also use 'VNC' for this.

The palm top devices are getting very good, but the screen is so small that it's hard to use for real work beyond e-mails.

Laptops are getting cheaper in price all the time, and you would only need a network card and/or a wireless card for access in most places.

Laptops now come with everything you need to connect to the 'AS400', except 'Client Access' and 'VPN'. Wireless networks are becoming more common, and it's very easy to connect from anywhere. Provided you have a good firewall and anti-virus program on the laptop, 'VPN' should give you a secure connection to the home network.

With the wireless connection of a laptop, you can connect anywhere. It's got to be the simplest and most flexible solution.

Question 45: P42045 Customer Service

I find out that if I call up and order the drill into 'Order Entry', it brings me to the 'Sales Detail' screen as expected. At the bottom screen, it lists "F15=SO Header" as an option, as well as it is listed as a valid function key on "F24". Some AR people that use the 'Customer Service' recently had a need to look at the 'Sales Header' for some information about the order. But "F15" didn't worked. In fact, it acted like an invalid function key. There was no error or anything. I looked at the code for "P42045", and I found that "F15" doesn't appear to have anything to do with going to the 'Sales Header'. I searched the 'KG' and found a few references to "F15" and "incorrect amounts when toggling".

I want to get to the 'Sales Header' from 'Customer Service' easily. How can I do that?

A: You can use 'JDE World A73.11'.

JDE Pristine Environment:
        Vocabulary Overrides: V42045, list for
Function Key Definitions:
        Display Text: "F15=Qty/Amount/Price".

        Function Key Descr: "Display Quantity,
Amount or Price Format
        15 #F02
        "Exit to Sales Ledger Inquiry
        15 #S13

You may want to determine if you are working with a modified version of the application (Pristine / Production / Custom).

You can try "P42045, list SOs, option 1 to V42113, <F15> to V4210" in version A7.3.10.

You can also check the following:

Sometimes the header records are not in sync between "F4201/F4211" and "F42019/F42119" because not all 'SO' detail lines get invoiced. Make sure that the underlying header record does exist. If it doesn't exist, then there will be no error message.

In "P42045", there is processing 'option 13' for the version name of "P4211". Make sure this "P4211" version is set up properly.

I recommend that the users should use "P42045" to get the document number and type, and then look up the 'SO' in "P4211". This may be overkill, but it also helps the user to remember to check that the desired data is still in the current files (F4201 & F4211) and not in the history files (F42019 & F42119).

You need to change the text for the "F15" key. Look at the JDE pristine environment to check what the text should be.

Question 46: World writer headers

We recently upgraded 'OS' to 'v5r3'. Prior to doing so, our 'world writers' came out with headers on the report, even if there were no detail records under them. Now, we do not get any headers unless we have some detail to print on the report. We are in A7.3.12

How can we fix this so that the headers will be displayed again?

A: You should have contacted JDE before upgrading to 'V5R3'.

There are a number of patches required for 'WW' as well as other back-office programs when upgrading to this version of the OS.

The white paper for the upgrade to 'V5R3' is "WST-04-0004.htm". You can search for it and find it on the 'peoplesoft.com' web site. There were applied 2 updates per JDE support, "6166870" which seems to pertain to 'World Writers', and "6417931" which seems to fix a decimal point error in inventory. Both were needed for 'V5R2' also. These are object code updates, not source code.

Question 47: V4R2 to V5R3

I'm planning to convert from 'V4R2' to 'V5R3'.

What should I watch for?

A: You are going to need to update World. It needs 2 sets of patches (I can't recall the JDE term) that replace about 8 program objects. JDE has white papers, and can find the information and code that is needed for the upgrade.

There are several SAR that need to be installed. Also, if you have any CL program that uses "CPYFRMIMPF", you may encounter problems, so use instead "CPYFRMSTMF".

Question 48: Sales Order Header Purge

We have our sales orders set to archive to the history files every night after sales update, so that our invoiced sales can all run from the history files (F42101, F42119). There is a large number of 'Sales Order Headers' still in "F4201" without detail lines in "F4211". However, there is no header in "F42019", but all the detail lines are in "F42119". We are using A7.3 cum 15.

Is there an easy way to get these order headers across from "F4201" to "F42019" without having to identify them and manually select them?

Is there an archiving program in World that might help with this?

A: There is a 'Standard Sales Order Header Purge Program P4201P' on 'Menu G42312'.
The Help Text states:

> "Running the Sales Order Header Purge"

Use the 'Sales Order Header Purge' to purge 'sales order header records' from the 'Sales Order Header' file. Records are purged from the 'Sales Order Header' file only, if no open detail lines with a matching order type. The order number combination exist in the 'Sales Order Detail' file. In addition to purging records, you can optionally move information to the 'Sales Order Header History' file. You can specify in the processing options whether you want to move an information.

You can purge 'sales order header' information from the 'Sales Order Header' file and move it to the 'Sales Order Header History' file during sales update.
JDE provide a lot of purge programs, most can be found using the 'Hidden Selection 27' from the appropriate system menu (e.g. G42 for Sales, G43 Purchasing, etc.).

There are special programs (like the one for Sales Order Header), but the majority use "PooPURGE". Test the 'Purge' thoroughly before you run in Production.

Question 49: Password Field

I am developing a stand alone application which have user authentication.

How will I handle the password field, so that it will show *** in place of alphanumeric?

A: if you are programming in 'RPG', and using 'SDA' or 'RDA' (for JDE), you should use the 'ND' (non display) attribute to the password field. This is the same property as when you are signing in to the 'AS400'.

If you are using developer tools, then you have to 'right click' on that field and change it to a password.

Question 50: Versions of World

What are the oldest and latest versions of World from the beginning?

A. The Company was founded in 1977, which focused on accounting software for the then booming Oil and Gas industry. The early S/38 versions from the mid 80's were named 'D', 'E', and 'F'.

OneWorld was released in 1995, at the same time that World version 'A73' was announced, so they called the 'OW' version 'B73'. "B7322" before XE was really named "B7333".

There are World versions A5.1, A5.2, A6.1, A6.2, A7.2, A7.3, and A81. Obviously A7.3 and A8.1 are still around. There were versions prior to A5.1.

Question 51: Password Encryption

Is there any documentation, or a way to determine if user passwords are encrypted for storage and/or transmission under AS/400-JDE?

A. On the AS/400 (iSeries) the user password is stored internally in encrypted form when it is created/changed - as far as I know there is no way to recover a user password. It is my understanding from IBM training years ago that when a user signs on, the Op System encrypts the entered password and compares it against the already stored encrypted password.

I do not know what happens between entry of the password on the screen (i.e. terminal/CRT or PC) and its arrival at the CPU - maybe it is transmitted "en clair" or maybe not. You would need to have deep and meaningful techno talks with IBM (and also the providers of your LAN/WAN network).

JDE Software doesn't do anything with passwords related to OS/400.

JDE does its own thing with the password (if used) for order hold and release (Sales Order and Purchasing Order processing) - this has nothing to do with the AS/400 and I believe it is not encrypted, just stored in a JDE file not normally accessible to the general user (requires menu or other security over access to P42090).

AS/400 passwords are stored encrypted. There is no way anyone, not even QSECOFR, can retrieve an AS/400 password. If someone forgets their password, you have to change the user profile and force them to change that temporary password the next time they sign on. If you want formal documentation, contact IBM support or go to the IBM publications web site and look for the AS/400 security manuals. This is an IBM thing - is not a JD Edwards thing.

Transmission could be a different story. Depending on what doing, AS/400 passwords could be transmitted unencrypted.

Question 52: Program Changes

I'm conducting an audit of general computer controls with regard to JDE. Our client produced a report (PGMRPT) for us to discern what programs have been modified. I found the following two entries:

```
Library......Object.........Created by User
---------+----------------+---------------+
JDFOBJ.......X0001M...........KD857311
EDTESTOBJ....P58L003..........JONDOE
```

Can someone define for me the objects, and let me know their significance?

A. That's part of the JDE menu system, and I'd be surprised if you have a source code for that as it's generally not released. The program has, or should have, no observability which means that JDE do not want you to look into it. License checking is performed somewhere within the menu system, so modifications to this program could be a sensitive issue.

I would restore the original X0001M from the JDE release tape to a temporary library and compare the two versions using both the DSPPGM and DSSPOBJD commands. In particular, check the object sizes, the creation date, the source file, and the source file change date/time. If the only differences are the change date and the save/restore information then I suspect all that happened is that someone ran the CHGPGM command over it, which would not actually alter the program's function. Even if it checks out I personally would restore the as-delivered version of X0001M over the changed one, having first copied it away somewhere in case I suddenly needed to put it back.

P58L003 is not a standard JDE program. System code 58 is reserved for client (i.e. your own) use. This is therefore a home-grown program. The interesting thing to me is that you have or had a user profile on the system call JONDOE. On a machine running an ERP system you want every user profile used to sign on to the system to be linked to a single identifiable person.

Question 53: Free Goods

When a customer buys item A he has an option to get either item B or item C free. I can set up Advanced Pricing so that when he buys A he automatically gets B free.

Is there a way to select which item must be added, as free goods, during sales order entry?

A. It would appear the functionality you are seeking is available from version 8.9 onwards.

The details below are from the Oracle paper 'Upgrade Value Proposition for JD Edwards OneWorld Xe to EnterpriseOne 8.11 SP1'.

"Free Goods Catalog (8.9)".

Free goods are frequently used in competitive industries such as consumer-packaged goods, to drive orders of a specific product. An example would be offering a free case of wine B to a customer that purchases ten cases of wine A. Obviously, customers that already have a big stock of wine B will hardly be motivated by this offer. However, if the company could offer customers a choice of three or four wines that can be taken for the free goods, the offer may be more enticing to the customer.

The free goods catalogue enhancement enables an organization to set up any number of free goods for the customer to choose from. During order entry, the system recognizes when an order or order line qualifies for a free good involving a catalogue of choices. The order entry person is notified and can review the choices with the customer. In automated order situations where there is no interaction, (such as EDI orders or store-and-forward orders) the free good that the organization sets up as the default will be selected by the system.

Remember that free goods don't actually have to be "free." They could be offered at a reduced price. For example, a deal could be defined as follows: Buy ten cases of wine A, and receive a case of either wine B or C for just $10. Note the price for each catalogue option needs to be the same, and the give-away cannot be split such as a half case of B and a half case of C. There can only be one item on a free goods line."

Question 54: Payable Voucher Post Status

Under what circumstances is the Payable Voucher Posted status showing "D"?

Under what circumstances is its posted status showing "P"?

A: If you have a P status on a voucher and no post process is currently running then I suggest you may have a problem. There should have been some sort of report from the post process or a joblog but it was probably too many days ago to find. Check the rest of the vouchers in the batch, if they show " " (blank) or "P" then reset the batch header status and run the post process again - make sure you watch the job through to completion then print the reports and review them. If there is still an error then these reports should tell you what it is.

Of course you should now read the User Reference Guide or make use of the cursor position sensitive "Help" key (F1) to find out what each of the values in "Posted Status" represent.

Question 55: Incorrect Monetary Text on an A/P check

We wrote an A/P check today for $21,000,000 and noticed that instead of printing text of "TWENTY ONE MILLION AND 00/100*********" that it printed "$21,000,000.00*********"? We have printed plenty of checks in the "millions" before, in fact I'm looking at a $3.5M check and the text is fine.

I'm afraid the bank won't process it because of the incorrect text. I scoured around the KG and found some instances of things related to problems with <$100M checks but nothing that stuck out as what is "wrong" with mine. Of course, I have posted a case with JDEPeoOrac to see what they wpould say about this.

In the meantime, is there anything I can do to correct the situation?

A: If the amount in words is too large to fit on the line or the call to the server program that converts an amount to words fails, JDE will print the amount instead. You may have to put logging on the check job or do a debug to find out which situation is causing your problem. I suspect it is the number of characters in words that is your problem. The issue is not per se the dollar amount - the issue is when you convert that dollar amount to words, that particular dollar amount may hit the character limit.

Something like 21,000,000 may work, but 21,788,888.88 may fail. You have to break the payment into multiple checks to get around the problem. Or pay JDE to fix it for you.

Question 56: Purchase Order Approvals

We are trying to do some testing on the purchase order approval process on our test system against a subset of data from production but we do not want to run the test through the entire approval route process. Does anyone know of a way to get around and reduce the approvals to be limited to the tester only? I noticed in the program P43080, that it can be run in Demo mode but I could not find anywhere in the documentation on how to set it up to run it in that mode.

What are my options?

A. Looking at the program it appears that the demo mode is invoked when the approval route code on the order matches the user's group profile on the User Information file F0092.

Normally the user's group or class has to begin with an asterisk so you will probably need to use DFU or some other utility to set it. Maybe World Writer (spit) could be used. Obviously the user will lose the functionality of his/her normal class or group while the record is set this way, so it may be worth creating a one-off user profile just for this.

I suspect it's intended for use by JDE's internal developers only, which might explain why it's not documented and why accessing it is ugly. I haven't tested this so can't guarantee it'll work, but it looks like it might be worth a shot.

Question 57: Deactivating Credit Hold for Sales Orders

We currently place customers of all our business units on credit hold when they go over the credit limit set in the Customer Master. For one BU we would like to turn off this feature. I know that it can be done customer by customer on screen 4206, but the help message for that function HINTS that credit hold can be turned off at the order entry level, which would be simpler and preferable:

".. credit checking is activated through the Sales Order Entry processing options "

However, I can find no instructions as to HOW one turns credit checking on and off in Sales Order Entry. I can guess it is done by not entering a credit hold code, but neither help nor the training guides discuss this.

We use separate versions of P4211 for each BU, so changing the option is feasible. Is this how it works?

A. In the P4211 Version for that Business Unit, don't set the Order Hold Code for Customer Credit Checking. That should release the hold.

Question 58: X091101 - F0911 File Server

How do I use this file server X091101 to UPDATE F0911 successfully?

I realized that in order to Update or Delete a record, you also have to pass the Relative Record order and member number.

How could we achieve that?

A. You can get the relative record number by linking the F0911 to the file information data structure (*INFDS) located in copy book I00SC via your "F" specs. As to the member, data files in World are single-member files. However, before you use this server, please double-check for any XF-prefix servers that may be applicable for file I/O. Please review the APCS (Advanced Programming Concepts and Skills) guide for examples of JDE server usage.

Another suggestion is you can find out how to use this file server by scanning your JDESRC file for a program that uses X091101, and use the logic you find to guide you. The info you seem to need (RRN and member number) are in the file information data structure. If you are not familiar with this, check out the RPG manuals on IBM's website.

Question 59: Importing foreign file into World for "Z' file process

Does anyone have any info on importing a foreign file into World Software for "Z" file process?

A. You can use to convert file in the text file upload in the database (DB2/400, sql-server). Soon after that, write a program or sql to upload in Z-files.

Question 60: FASTR Downloads on menu

I have created some FASTRs which are on % menus so they can be run overnight but the clients want to download them to txt files to use in Excel. They can drag and drop through Ops navigator but they want download files. Is there any way of taking option 8 on a FASTR from a menu option so the download files can also be submitted overnight? If this can be done, then it's just a case of creating a dos batch file to download them all to the PC.

A: In the FASTR specs, you indicated you want to create a download file. So why not just create the file when a person runs the FASTR? Pop up the little screen that comes up when you do the '8' when they run the report and have everything done in one run.

By the way, the job it runs is J/P83091 when you do your '8' so you must have to have pass various parms (version, member, etc) so it might not be pretty to try and "automate".

When you select option 8 it first calls the windowing program P83OPT5 to set the parameters. This program simply sets processing options 36 to 42 in the DreamWriter Master Parameter file F98301. These remain set, so if you have run option 8 once manually, and the parameters are the way you want them, you can omit this step.

It then runs P83300 which actually submits the J/P83091 job to create the download file. To simulate P83300 all you have to do is call J00BTCH2 with 4 parameters. These are:

1. 'J83091 ' (length 10)
2. FASTR Form ID (length 10)
3. FASTR Version (length 10)
4. Return code (length 1)

Question 61: Defining default user business unit

I need to define the default business unit for a new employee so that for example, in Sales Order Entry, the orders they give will enter default to a given business unit. However I cannot find the program where you set this up, either by searching menus or searching by keyword.

I am also having trouble finding the menu options. I thought it was under the Default Location & Printers, but other users who have a default are not listed in there, so there must be something else in addition. How do I fix this?

A. It should be in the default Location & Printers. If you want to verify, search the source for P4211 for 40095 and see what the test is around the lines that have this search value.

Type the word "Default" and hit F8. This should bring up the list with "Default Location & Printers." Then you can select the menu option with either a 4 or 5. I typically use a 5 and go to the menu instead of executing the option blind as it was. (Of course you have to have the Menu Word Search refreshed, J980090, about once a week to keep up with menu changes.)

You may also want to try F6 from the User Information Page 0092. It says "company use only" but that might be what you are seeing as a default for the users with no Default locations & Printers data.

Question 62: Create PF in SVR - Additional Parameters

I believe something is wrong when creating a PF in SVR. The file Once ...
OVRDBF FILE(F56SSM) SHARE(*YES) ... in CL cannot be Access by the RPG program. It comes up with dump message – "File is already OPEN or there is an error".

I thought it was the Dream Writer Specifications. However, I want to be sure it is not caused by the "Additional Parameters" when creating PF.

What can I do to resolve this?

A. If you are running this program interactively I think the most likely reason for the error message is that it is telling you the truth and the file is already open within your job.

This message often occurs when you are testing an RPG program under Dream Writer interactively, possibly in debug mode. If for any reason the program terminates abnormally, the next time you try to run it, you'll get this message.

To fix this, you can try the following steps in the following order:

1. Simply run it again. Often the file gets closed as the error message is generated.

2. Explicitly close the file from the command line using CLOF F56SSM.

3. The old favorite: sign off and on again. This usually works although it can be a bit of a pain.

Some points for clarification though:

1. You only need to do a CLOF when you explicitly open the file in the CL, usually with a shared open data path and OPNQRYF. In JDE this nearly always means you are running under

DreamWriter, and the JDE standard CL code usually does a good job of tidying up after itself. You can generate a standard CL program yourself by running the Quick Start CL Generator from menu G93/5.

2. You should really be running these jobs in batch, so it normally doesn't actually matter that much if the files get left open at job end as the open data paths disappear with the job.

3. This problem occurs quite frequently in testing as the programmer runs the DreamWriter interactively in order to use the interactive debugging facilities. If the programmer terminates the program using the debugger the CLOF in the CL gets bypassed anyway, so it doesn't really help. The answer in this situation when debugging is to close the file explicitly by executing a CLOF from the command line.

Question 63: Missing columns in JDE 8.11 for F4211 and F42119

I have to convert an existing data warehouse extraction routine from our B733 system to a new 8.11 system. Some columns seem to have disappeared in these two tables F4211 and F42119.

These columns are:

```
SDBALU,
SDPSDJ,
SDDSPR,
SDDSFT,
SDFAPP,
SDPRMO,
SDDFTN,
SDCDCD,
SDCOT,
SDAFT,
SDFUF1,
SDFRTC,
SDFRAT,
SDRATT,
SDCMGL,
SDSTTS,
```

```
SDSLSM,
SDSLCM,
SDSLM2,
SDSLC2,
SDANI,
SDAID,
SDOMCU,
SDOBJ,
SDSUB,
SDLT
```

How do I remedy the situation?

A: Make sure in your CL that you specify CLOF <Filename> before it finishes. What OS400 is trying to tell you is that the file is already open and it is set to share its path. If you try to open it

again it will fail. If you get this message while in the interactive session issue CLOF <filename> and you will get over this problem. In normal situation in your CL you should do CLOF before ending the CL.
F42119 is a flex file. You get to choose some of the columns (fields) that go into that file.

There is a program to create the flex file. I would guess there are a bunch of warns about when you should and shouldn't change the file.

I would advise read, re-read, ask question and then proceed cautiously before changing the flex files.

Question 64: Showcase query

Has anyone use the feature in SHOWCASE Query that will allow you to select from a list of values in a PC File?

What we are trying to do is to select records from F0911 that have a matching batch number in an Excel Spreadsheet. But we can't get it to work. We first tried formatting the cells in the spread sheet as numeric, then as text (with leading zeros) but nothing is working.

What are we doing wrong?

A: In the query conditions, select the prompt (under Expression), then under source of prompt, select from the drop down list > "list of values from a pc file;
Then you can browse to an xls spreadsheet file.

Question 65: Inserting data into Z-Tables

Could you please tell me how data is inserted into Z-Tables? How are they being processed after inserting data in Z-tables?

A. The Z table should be fed by data from some 3rd party s/w. The data processing should be exactly like that of One World Xe.

Question 66: Outer Join in World Writer

How do you perform an outer join on two files in World Writer? It seems the only join we can do is an equal join.

A. You'll have to use query for that or ODBC with MS Access. This may not be functional in WW but it is found in many other reporting packages and Query.

Question 67: Log of running applications

How can I find which application was running? How many times has P4210, for example, ran and from which user?

A: There is a World file, F0082H, which contains menu history records. This file is not perfect for usage reporting, but it is a start. From menu G94, there is a Menu History option, you can get the information you require there.

F0082 is Menu Master and F0082H is Menu Selection History. F0082H is the one to look at if you want to see what people have been doing.

Question 68: Sales Taxes and Sales Orders

Recently, Idaho went from 6% to 5% tax. We changed the tax tables accordingly, retiring the old rate and creating the new one.

We found that if we have an order with an Order Date of pre-7/1 (tax date change) the items were not shipped until AFTER 7/1, it calculates the tax based on the Order Date, not the Ship or Invoice Date.

For example: I have an order dated 6/20 with one line item that gets backordered. The item comes in a month later and we ship it and complete the order (day end). The Order date is 6/20 and the Ship/Invoice/GL dates are all 7/21 at this point. When it creates the AR/GL entries, the tax is calced at 6% (pre 7/1) instead of 5% (post 7/1). It appears that tax is calculated on the Order Date only and I can't find "why" that happened. I assumed it would be something in P42800 but I can't find any processing option that changes that practice.

How can I turn this around?

A: My first question is - are you sure that the rate is set up properly in F4008? I have a bug in P4008 which makes it very cumbersome to enter new rates - but it does eventually get it right. Query the table to make sure that it is set up properly.

There are several dates in F4211 and I'm not sure exactly which date is used to calculate the sales taxes. I know that there is a promised ship date (SDPPDJ) and an actual ship date (SDADDJ).

The upload file F4001Z calculates sales taxes using the transaction date (SYDRQJ) so I suspect that maybe SDDRQJ in F4201 is the date used to calculate the rate.

We had a similar problem when adding Bills/Routers for work orders that already existed (i.e. the Item and WO's were created before we got around to creating Bills). By default, the "Effective

From" date is set to "Today", therefore if you try to start a WO with a date earlier than today it will not attach the parts list.

My point is that if there is an Effective Date for the new Tax Rate and all transactions for the old rate have now been posted, can you change the "Effective From Date" for the Tax Rate so that this covers older orders.

Question 69: Uploading Data in WorldSoft

How do I upload data in WorldSoft?

A. JDE has provided a method of importing data into their system for most transactional and some setup tables. It's generally called the z-file process, as the table that you load data into is named with the same name as the transactional file, but with a Z1 at the end, so, for instance, the file that you would load for importing data into the F0411 is named F0411Z1. The JDE process takes the data that you have loaded into F0411Z1, does the edits and processes the data into the real F0411. So your job is to upload data into the F0411Z1 (for AP vouchers). You can upload data into the file in various ways. For instance, client access comes with a file transfer mechanism or you can ftp the data from your PC into a table, making sure that you use a correct translation command as the data on a PC is in ASCII format while the AS/400 holds data in EBCDIC format.

Depending on which data you are uploading there is a different Z-file and process to use. You can usually find these types of processes on the Advanced or Technical menus, options 27/29 from the menu. Type "Help" and the option number to get more information.

Question 70: DreamWriter Variable

We have a DW driven RPG program that we need to process 1 of 3 files (the entire same format).

I know that you can specify the physical file name as the "Based On
File" in the Additional Parameters, but how can you change this when the
RPG program has a single file name?

Do you have to make the File Output Type "2" and then copy it to a file of the same name in the RPG, or is there a simpler way to do this?

A: Sounds like an OVRDBF (override data base file) command in the CL would work. However be very careful if the CL program is calling the P98815 program to do the Open Query file. Not sure if the OVRDBF to another file name will work with the OPNQRYF function in JDE. You would have to test that. You could be safer just copying the appropriate file to some work file and using that work file all the time for the RPG program, assuming not big files have to be copied.

If you have a source handy, look at J/P04423 from vanilla JDE. This is an A/P detail report that will either go over the F0411JC or F0411AJC file (as of or not) and uses the "based on" file to drive things. I'm pretty sure it is just like your example. There is a Processing Option on it as well that tells whether to use the "As Of" file. My guess is the CL retrieves the option value and uses OVRDBF to get the right file.

It might be just easiest to use a work file (as suggested) and have your RPG run over the work file. You would still need a proc. opt to tell it which file to copy into the work file though.

Question 71: Calculating days

I am trying to write a query in Query/400 on the F4211 file where SDTRDJ is less than today's date + 3 days (NOT counting the weekends).

Is there a way to do this in a query?

A: You will need a workday calendar table. For a while our fiscal year did not match the calendar year and we had holidays as well to consider. The only solution I could come up with at the time was to build a calendar table. One of the columns in my calendar table was a running workday total. I also had the normal Julian in a column and the JDE Julian in a column. You could add a column to get the desired return date based upon the JDE Julian you mention below. The only problem we had was with actual workdays since we occasionally worked Saturdays. This was especially hard since sometimes they wanted the reporting by department. The only way we could do that was through code. I personally found it easiest to create the calendar in Excel, and then import it to the AS/400 and set the key over the JDE Julian column.

This is another suggestion that can be done in SQL:

```
SELECT * FROM F4211

WHERE STDRDJ > CURRENT_DATE + 3 DAYS

AND DAYOFWEEK(STDRDJ) > 1
```

The final solution that is presented is using a query that you can define the following result fields:

Define Result Fields

Type definitions using field names or constants and operators, press Enter.
Operators: +, -, *, /, SUBSTR, ||, DATE...

Field Expression Column Heading Len Dec

SDDATE date(
'20'||substr(digits(SDTRDJ),2,5))

TODAY CURRENT(DATE)

DIFFERENCE DAYS(SDDATE) - DAYS(TODAY)

You will then be able to make the following selections :

Select Records

Type comparisons, press Enter. Specify OR to start each new group.
Tests: EQ, NE, LE, GE, LT, GT, RANGE, LIST, LIKE, IS, ISNOT...

AND/OR Field Test Value (Field, Number, 'Characters', or ...)
SDTRDJ NE 0
AND DIFFERENCE LE 3
AND DIFFERENCE GE 0

This does not help with the exclusion of weekends but it does enable you select SDTRDJ where it is less than today + 3 days.

Question 72: Unable To license User

When our user signs on to JDE environment A73.cum11, they got "Unable to License User. Try Again Later". Our operators have to terminate their session. Then they signed back on and got in.

What is the cause of this message?

A: That means you have exceeded the maximum amount of user allowed to be signed on to JDE. If you go to Menu G943 take option 3 . Audit/Error Message Inquiry:

98806 Audit/Error Message Inquiry Msg Filter . . *ALL

Maximum Users Allowed. . 60

Times Limit Exceeded . . . 5 Last Exceeded Date. . . . 10/04/04

Starting Date . . . . . . 07/06/05 Ending Date 07/06/05

Starting Time . . . . . . 08:00:00 Ending Time 15:00:00

User Name . . . . *ALL Device Name . . . . *ALL

Date Time MSG Message Description

07/06/05 3203 Maximum user count reached was 00040. Here Maximum Users Allowed is 60.

Find documents on the Software License Manager. The licenses are reset by a job that can be setup in either the system startup or put into a nightly job as long as users are not signed on when it runs. Support can give this information to you.

It's also possible that your SLM indexes are corrupted. Have you had a power failure recently where your system went down? I had a situation last year where the indexes used by the SLM (software license manager) were damaged and this skewed the count for users logged on. Perhaps you can try the Support desk for instructions on how to clear them and re-initialize the SLM. The SLM manual reviews this process on pages 2-1 through 2-4.

Question 73: ODBC Connection fails

I am trying to use Access to export some data from SYS7333_F00950 and when I try to connect, I get the following error message:

```
ODBC -- call failed
[IBM][Client Access Express ODBC Driver (32-
bit)][DB2/400 SQL]SQL5016 - Qualified object name
'F00950' not valid. (#-5016)
```

After we click on OK it gives us this message:

Microsoft Access can't open the table in Database view.

I am able to connect to PRDDTA_F0001 and export data from it. The only difference that we have been able to find is under DSPFD under record format the F00950 is set as F00950 and the F0001 is set to I0001. Could this be our problem? What is the "I" and "F" types? We have also been able to connect to other tables that have "I" under the record format.

How can we fix this?

A. About the "F" and "I", it is a convention with JDE to name the file with the Fxxyyy and the record format with Ixxyyy. (xx = System code and yyy is the group code). So looking at the file ID, 00 would be the World Foundation Environment and group code 950 would be Housekeeping.

The F00950 was generated from OneWorld using SQL. The F0001 was compiled for World using AS400 DDS source. F0001 is in a native DB2 format while the F00950 is standard SQL. You are able to access DB2 tables with SQL.

That being said, I'm not sure why you are having a problem accessing Foo950 from Access. Check the data source you are using.

Question 74: FASTR total rounding

I have a problem with the totals on Row spec FASTRs. The figures are in round thousands so I don't want to display decimals but the totals are the totals of rounded figures. E.g. if you had 10499 on one row and -9501 on the next it rounds to 10 - 10 and the total is 0 whereas the actual figure gives a difference of 998 which when rounded to thousand equals 1. Overall the rows this can lead to significant differences by the last row.

Is there any way of forcing the totals to be the actual total rounded rather than the rounded figures totaled?

A: You will need to have a non-display cell to hold the total value for the row with all the decimal places needed to keep from rounding, and then move that to a display cell rounded to thousands for the report. You may be able to do this with a column instead of individual cells, depending on how your FASTR is defined.

For more information you can check-out the FASTR reference guide (A7.3) pages 6.1-6.2 and the reference to "Recalculation", also pages 6.6-6.7. You might need cell calcs for your totals.

Question 75: Calculating the total pages

Is it possible to print total pages on the page header? I know printing the current page is easy, but I don't know how to print total page in the page header. I need such format: Current Page/ Total Page. Is that possible?

A: Not really. The problem is that the pages are being produced, you do NOT know how many total pages there will be. You would like to generate and get a count, then somehow go through a second process to regenerate the report with the Total pages.

What you could do is send the report through a forms software package, which should handle that kind of thing. If you really need a total page count to show on each page, that is the best direction to go in.

Question 76: FASTR Balance Auditor files

Files F8308/F8310 in the Common Library is 2 GB and 12 GB respectively.
Both are multi-member files and described as "FASTR Balance Auditor".

Can these be re-organized in any way?

A: The Balance auditor should only be used where really necessary as it not only creates very large files (as you have found out) but also slows down the FASTRs.

You might find that people don't even know they are creating them. If this is the case the FASTRs can be changed and the members deleted.

The balance auditor files are supposed to be purged automatically by JDE about two days after they are created.

You can "reorganize" the balance auditor files but it would best be done using IBM commands, firstly though you have to find the FASTR versions that create/update these members and make some decisions whether or not these should continue to do so.

Very few (if any) reports should be creating balance auditor files on a regular basis.

My suggested approach, which depends on your relationship with your users and your site rules (i.e. adapt my approach to suit yourself):

1. Make sure you have last night's backup just in case there is a user who has been using the Balance Auditor files to store a "point in time" report by account. Use CLRPFM to clear all the members in the balance auditor files, and then run a RGZPFM. This will get back disk space fast. Don't worry; they will get updated as needed next execution of any FASTR with auditor turned on.

2. Use QRY etc to identify all FASTR definitions that have the Override
Default for balance auditor turned on. Take a quick look at the file with QRY or SQL will help you find out. Make a list out of the versions.

3. Have the users review all these versions on your list and have them identify and justify those that are really necessary.

4. While the users are about this task, use DSPFD to an "outfile" (you need to check the parms because you want details about each member) – use this outfile to identify all the ones that have an "old" last used/changed date. If there are a lot of old members then decide on a nice cutoff date. Write a simple CL to read through the outfile and execute RVMBR. This will clear all the old stuff en masse and get some more space back but run your reorganization again.
5. When the users get back to you with their list - use RVMBR to knock off the rest of the problematic members, then, go into FASTR and change the override defaults (or use WW in update mode).

Question 77: Changes on FASTR

When one of our power users (with more authority than regular users) makes a change to a FASTR Heading or Description, this change is not reflected when a regular user runs the Fastr. However, when a regular user makes the same change to the FASTR, all users can see the modified heading or description. The power user would like to make changes on headings and have those changes shown on the FASTR run by others.

How can we implement this?

A. Firstly, are your library lists set correctly for the "power users" - i.e. is the LIBL the same as that used by the "regular users"? Please double (triple) check and then once the "power user" is signed on and in FASTR, you should use DSPJOB USER ("power user") from another session (workstation) and make sure what files are coming from what libraries.

Secondly, check all this against what the "regular user" gets. Maybe the power user is signed into a CRP or some sort of training/playground environment and doesn't realize it. Then check the FASTR set ups and make sure the "power user" is not changing a test version and that there are no column/row overrides etc. that could confuse the problem. Maybe what the power user is changing is not what is used during execution time.

Question 78: Default AS400 Output Queue

Instead of chaining to F0092 to get the Output queue, is there any other way to get it by means of calling an external program in RPG.

What is the name of the program or command that is called by HS 39?

A. You will probably need to call a CL program with a parameter to do a
RTVJOBA command and retrieve the output queue value for the job and pass it back to the RPG program.

Question 79: Data exchange between Oracle DB and JD Edwards

We have an Oracle 10g database which we maintain. The financial system is using JD Edwards. We need to provide them some daily information (payments) They also need to send us some data (payment reconciliation).

My questions are:

1. What kind of interaction is possible between Oracle db and JD Edwards?
2. What database does JD Edwards internally use? Is in an Oracle db?
3. Is there an ODBC driver available for interaction?
4. Does JD Edwards handle credit card payments?

A: Your questions are answered accordingly:

1. You can't get there directly, but you can get there through Java/JDBC. You can write some programs that use a trigger on a JDE file that feeds a data queue that feeds a Java program that uses a JDBC connection into an Oracle db.

2. DB2. Oracle is not available natively on the iSeries.

3. Yes, you can use ODBC or JDBC but the connection is the least of the problem. What you have to figure out is how to process the information on either end.

4. The iSeries - AS/400 - i5 systems use DB2/400, which is a platform-specific version of the DB2 database.

Here are some options:

1) Continue using FTP;

2) The Oracle Transparent Gateway for DB2/400 is an expensive piece of software (IIRC, ~25,000.00 US) that you can buy from Oracle that that gives you a DRDA connection between the iSeries (AS/400) and Oracle. Once installed, you can write

iSeries applications in High-Level Languages like RPG that can send and retrieve data directly to/from Oracle tables;

3) Write an iSeries Java application that uses JDBC to read and write data from/to the Oracle database. However, I'm not sure how viable this option is with V5R1, and depending on the model and amount of memory in your iSeries machine you could cause some performance problems by using Java;

Question 80: FASTR Edit codes

Is it possible to create custom edit codes?

I want to print % but only on certain lines and the % format prints zero balances. What I would like is a similar code to % but without zero balances.

I tried using a BL column type with cell overrides for the cells I want but that doesn't work so I have to use a % column and zero out the ones I don't want.

Am I reduced to using Edit code M and not having the trailing % sign?

A: You can create a system-wide edit code since you are running on AS/400. The command is CRTEDTD (Create Edit Description).

It turns out that program X00162 does the editing for FASTR values. However, the source code for this program is not shipped to customers, and JDE Tech. It's an ASM (assembler) program. There does not appear to be any way to use a custom edit code for FASTR reports.

Question 81: World Upgrade to CUM 15

I've been asked to upgrade from 11 to 15. Com library is shared between Test Environment and Production. Production is not to be touched in any way while upgrading the Test Environment.

So in the past I would have just copied COM to COMTEST and pointed the Test environment to COMTEST, then do the upgrade over the test environment.

Am I doing the right thing?

A: I just completed a load of CUM 15 to a development environment. What you need to do is specify separate common, security and data libraries for whatever environment you are upgrading - then run a single plan. CUM 15 does update all three library types. So, by all means copy COM and keep it for the upgrade to Test. Be sure to modify your lib lists to reflect the change. Be sure that your plan reflects the new common library. You also might want to check to see if you have access in the Test environment with the USERID you intend to use in Test, before you do the upgrade.

Question 82: Calculating days between 2 Julian dates

I need to calculate the days between two Julian dates.

Is there some AS400 Function or JDE function I can use?

A: I believe you are looking for X0035 for a difference between dates. X0027 is another handy JDE subprogram that allows you to increment a date by a requested number of days.

Question 83: Print version

There is a print question in our system. Dream write report P04413 has many versions. Some version will print to printer device directly without spool file when using, some version have spool file if used. I compared these two kinds of versions. The additional parameters are all the same.

Is there some other place that will set the print device?

I think the versions share the same RPG file and PRINT file, but where should the difference be in the setting for each version?

A: Until proven otherwise all Dream Writer reports produce a "spool file".

The actual report will be printed according to the printer OUTQ specified on the Dream Writer. Check your JDE User Reference
Guides - COMMON foundation - Work with Print Options (A7.3 page 9-32).
In very simple terms, if no OUTQ is specified on the DWV then the default
is basically what is defined on the USSPRF.

From memory, failing that it is the default associated with the WRKSTN the user is using. Then finally it goes back to a system parameter (one of the QSYSVAL parameters or something like that).

All this is pretty basic AS/400 (iSeries) stuff. There are many ways to determine what prints go where.

JDE gives you some limited choices at the specific DWV level, then you need to fall back to standard AS/400 (iSeries) protocols.
Another suggestion is to check the Option 6 by the version gives the Printer overrides.

Question 84: IBAN

Does anyone use IBAN for international payments? The only documentation I can find on the Oracle website says the functionality has been included in V8.9 and in the above.

If anyone uses these where do you store the information in JDE?

A: This functionality is being added as part of maintenance and will be released in Cume 16.

Question 85: One World to World

I realize that this is a pretty generic question but I might move to a company that uses World and my experience has only been with One World (XE).

What are the major differences that I should be aware of?

A: About the only thing the same are the tables underlying the software. Most of the applications, if they are coexistent, will also show/allow update of the same information.

World is an emulation software program, which only runs on the iSeries. The iSeries uses library lists to determine where the information can be found, vs. using Data Sources and OCM.

A World use signs onto a Client Access (or other terminal emulation software) and signs on interactively (this can be a performance difference) vs. using the ODBC jobs QZDASOINIT to connect.

There is only 1 user id setup for World, vs. a OneWorld user and its related back end System user. The user setup programs are remarkably similar. It is Menu G94 instead of GH9011.

World is written in RPG vs. C++/OneWorld RDA. The World specification tables include the DDS for the form as well as JDE tables which hold 'soft-coding'.

World use SVR - Software Versions Repository - instead of RDA. SVR uses IBM program PDM interface for writing and compiling code. This IBM program is not necessary if using OneWorld.

The user does not get configurable grids with World, the inquiries are static. The user cannot export straight out of a grid; they must use either IBM's file transfer or a 3rd party product.

Reports have versions in World, just like OneWorld, though the user's password does not show up in the job log for a World report like it does for a UBE.

Question 86: Report on F4311 and F43121

Have anyone tried to tie the PO file (F4311) and the Receiving file (F43121) on one report? We are able to do so; however when we have multiple receiving our original PO amount record is duplicated by the # of receiving. And we would like to show the original PO amount. Without having to resort to programming or Crystal I am just wondering if and how anyone was able to overcome this on a world writer. We are using a SQL view as our base file, similar to a logical function.

So how can I resolve the issue?

A: Well, if you do not want to total the original PO amount, you could specify that column value to only print when changed and should only print first time (though if the same amount right next to each other on the report for different PO lines, that would not work so good).

When joining to the F43121, you have to be careful which match type records you want as well. Otherwise that will also be a cause of multiple records, not just having multiple receipts on the same line.

Question 87: JDE Process Flows & Segregation of Duties

I need to be able to show a segregation of duties. This is so that, for example, I can prove that someone who raises a Purchase Order cannot write a cheque. The way I thought of going about it was to create a full process flow documentation in terms of JDE program and then using security reporting to prove that a user cannot access the conflicting parts of that flow.

We use Aquila software to manage our JDE security and for reporting.

How can we do this

A: Several years ago I wrote and uploaded a utility that may be a starting point for your search. It's called User/Program/Menu Cross Reference and is a variable from the download portion of the site. =0D=0A=20=0D=0ADouglas Belcher=0D=0AKV Pharmaceutical=0D=0ASt Louis, MO=0D=0AOpinions expressed are not necessarily those of my employer=20=0D=0A=0D=0A;

As JDE has standard programs called in every single program, consider the option of including the relationship between the users and the functions and validate the duties in one of those standard programs in order you don have to change all the JDE programs, just the one which is called in all the others.

Question 88: DW Versions Disappearing

Has anyone had any problems with versions disappearing after recursive versions has been activated?

We turned P43500 (PO Print) into a recursive 3 weeks ago, and since that some of the versions keep getting deleted. My boss decided to lock down option 9 so that nobody (at all!) can delete versions, but it's still happening.

The version names are of the format O_PO_110 or O_PO_110R (reprint) and from the job logs I can see that no attempt is made to delete these in the CL for one of the PO Prints. The sequencing of recursive versions also has come nowhere close to the names that we are using, plus of course if a version is recursive, the Form is set to +P43500 not P43500.

A. I haven't had this problem, but one is a way to identify how the DW versions are disappearing is to start journaling on the F98301 and f98302 files (see menu G9641).

Then, once you see a version that has "disappeared" again, go review the journal entries for the disappeared version and see what program deleted them from the files.

BTW, I have a fairly simple RPG program that you can modify in about 10 minutes to convert the journal entries from a given file into an arrival sequence database file so you can query the data and more easily identify the inserted/changed/deleted records.

This is something to do with the program P98310 (the Dream Writer Copy Version) and it is related to how a version is named. We get a DUMP when we name a version in the format 301_SO. We solved the problem by renaming our versions using different format.

As someone else said, if you journalize the F98301 file you can see all the operations (ADD, DELETE, CHANGE) applied to your DW versions, then you can identify user, program, date and time when your version was deleted.

You can review that information in order to identify the origin of the problem.

Question 89: JDE Account Reconciliation Tool

We have recently used the JDE account reconciliation tool to automate our bank reconciliations using bank tape reconciliation method and our 7543 account via a manual reconciliation.

I would now like to extend the use of this tool to other general ledger accounts. However my documentation on this function states something like "you can reconcile bank accounts, selected expense accounts, and other general ledger accounts in the General Accounting system".

Where can I get a more general overview of this functionality's limitations?

A: In the JDE reference guide "General Accounting" under the major heading of "Periodic Operations", there is a section titled "Account Reconciliation". The text (including diagrammatic detail) contained in this section should answer most of your questions. Your IT people should have a softcopy (or hard copy) version of this manual and should also be able to assist you.

For further detail, review the JDE setups your organization already uses for bank account reconciliations and account 7543 reconciliation, and then discuss with some experienced users within your organization.

I suspect you are correct - sounds like all you might need to do is extend what is already in use to apply it to other accounts.

Question 90: Accounts Payable and Bank Account Change

We have recently changed our bank. I have set up new bank account records in A/P in Bank Account Information (P04130) and a new G/L account for it as well.

I have changed the A/P AAI's to reflect the new default bank account and also the Create Payment Groups DreamWriter to pick up this bank account cheques and BACS payments.

The problem I have is that all the existing open items (logged and/or approved) that are waiting for payment were default coded to the old G/L bank account at the time of entry.

The only way I can find to amend this is to go into Speed Release and change each open voucher in the fold area. This is a massive task given the size of our open A/P ledger.

Does anyone know of a program within JDE to update this globally?
Failing this I'll be forced to revert to the Dangerous Utility route.

What are my alternatives?

A: You can do the following:

a) Use WW in update mode to change the bank account ref on the F0411 records for OPEN items only - you need to know how to use WW in update mode and how to identify records with an OPEN amount. This may be a problem for later cancelled/voided items (including cheques).

b) Use the "override bank account" processing option in the payment process - from memory it requires that you nominate the account ID (i.e. the eight digit internal JDE account reference for you new bank account - not the usual BU.OBJ.SUB) also known as the short account ID. But you need to enter it as an eight character value with leading zero's and no preceding "*" which (at A7.3 cum 9) was what it defaulted to if you use the F1 lookup from the proc option. From memory you need to define this override account in the "Create Payment Group" process (somewhere about Proc Option 13 through 15) - I can't remember any need to further to specify it but please check your cheque print functions as well.

Another suggestion is you can use Speed Release to globally update to your new bank account. Inquire on the old bank account, "C" to change, type the new account over the old account in the header and hit F6 for global update. That should change all your open vouchers to the new account.

Using the override bank account approach through payment processing also is more comprehensive in that if a cheque on the "old" bank account is voided then the related vouchers will be made "OPEN" again but of course will still have the "old" bank account reference. If these "reopened" vouchers are to be paid on a new cheque from the "new" bank account (as opposed to being voided themselves) the override bank account approach will work fine. Ultimately the problem should go away as the likelihood of voided cheques on the "old" bank account diminishes to zero. Now if you have multiple bank accounts in use then you need to do some deeper analysis/research to fully address the problem - probably set up multiple DWV's for payment processing.

Question 91: Sleeper submission anomaly

Has anyone ever seen a situation where Sleeper appears to submit a job but there is no job log and the job does not appear to have run?

We seem to be getting problems with several jobs, where no evidence of the job having been run can be found, yet the Sleeper log shows it as having been submitted.

These are operations jobs under the ID of IS staff, not user jobs.

All jobs / user profiles are set to produce job logs.

Our IS manager was also dismissed a few weeks ago. Hopefully nothing got changed in the Sleeper programs.

How can we fix this?

A: Look at the QHST log (DSPLOG) on the 400 to see what messages you see for the jobs. You should see a "submit" and a "completed" entry for the job(s) here.

You can also check "who" (user profile) is used to submit the jobs in question in Sleeper. Has anything happened to that user profile? You might change the logging level on that profile to spit out logs even if all goes well. In JDE user security, set the logging severity to 10 and the messages to *SECLVL. They are likely set to 00 and *NOLIST right now.

Question 92: AS400 JDE OneWorld full system backup

Our IT "shuts down" the AS400 OneWorld system every weekend for a full system backup for hours. We are told this is to maintain the data integrity and to speed up the backup. Is this truly necessary? It seems a bit strange that a system like AS400 still needs to be "shut down" (or kill all the sessions) to do the backup nowadays. If this is true, are there other third party apps available to do online backups without needing to shut down the system?

A: Well, this is the World list, not the OneWorld list, but the same applies to both. If, by a full system backup, you mean a SAVSYS (Save system) as well as saving all user libraries on the system and saving security and configuration information, then yes the AS/400 needs to bring down all system activity to do the full system save/backup. However the system only is required to be "down" during the Save System, Save Security, and Save Configuration parts of the backup. For user library backups, those saves can be done with a Save While Active function. However if your IT group is doing the IBM Save Full System option, then the system is going to be down during the entire process. I do not know of anyone who does the IBM Save Full System option because of that situation, but maybe it is happening for you. If the IBM stuff is not changing much, you could consider doing a full IBM system backup once a month instead of once a week. But certainly from a disaster recovery standpoint, once a week is a lot better.

To summarize, though the system does need to be "down" to users for the IBM backup stuff, it should not be down for hours (unless you are fortunate to have no one needing to use the system at the time). It sounds like the backup process needs to be restructured to reduce the down time.

There are other options, such as a backup using the save-while-active feature, but I am not convinced that restoring data from this type of backup would ensure data integrity, and it also significantly slows down any processing (online and batch). The last I knew (V5R1), this option still puts a lock on every file in the library it is backing up, which also causes conflicts for users on the system.

Other options to consider in lieu of the system shut down are:

1) Use IBM journaling for every file in your production and source code libraries, with the journal receivers set up in a separate ASP. However, this requires significant additional disk space (read: $$). Restoring your production data from journal receivers is neither easy nor straightforward.

2) Have a completely separate AS/400 and purchase software that will mirror the data in real time between the two systems, and then you run your backups from the 2nd machine. This works really well, but, you are talking big $$ to purchase additional hardware as well as software, and it takes some sophisticated setup and ongoing administration.

Question 93: Problem with reposting/rebuilding balance file

The problem is that we changed the GL date in one entry in GL (also period and fiscal year). It's connecting with changing FY from 5 to 4 (May to April) and then we rebuild balances (Ledger type AA and AU) (P099102) for all year to be sure that all is correct.

For FY 3, 4 and 5 all entries (balances) are correct in AA and AU ledger type.
the problem is with fiscal year 2 (first FY in company)- for this year Balance for AA was rebuild correctly, but ledger AU wasn't rebuild at all.

I think that because 2 is first year in company it can produce error - but what does it mean? And in old version ledger AU existed in F0902.

Second question is, is it the normal way that rebuilding of AA ledger type is not dependent of clearing F0902? When I try to rebuild the AU ledger type - if I delete AA ledger from F0902 - AA and AU are rebuilding, and if I don't delete existing AA - only the AA are rebuilding. Why is this?

How do we resolve these?

A: If you have access to knowledge garden could you check if there are something about P099102 , subroutine STL2:

(at the begginnig os Subr)

Set flag for not running units if only the currency code changes. There is no CRCD for Unit ledgers so we run through this logic too much without this flag.

```
*INL1 IFEQ *ON
GLSBL CABNE$4SBL ENDL1
GLSBLT CABNE$4SBLT ENDL1
GLCRCD IFNE $4CRCD
MOVE *ON $NORUN 1 Don't run Units

ELSE
```

```
MOVE  *BLANKS  $NORUN
ENDIF
ENDL1 TAG
MOVE  GLSBL  $4SBL
MOVE  GLSBLT  $4SBLT
MOVE  GLCRCD  $4CRCD
ENDIF
```

The problem is that for one account $CRCD is always blank for first read record from F0911 - so NORUN flag is always set ON, so always for first AID ledger type AU is not creating. IMO it should be also condition to check also that $CRCD is not blank (or any other checking for first read record).

Question 94: Creating Batch Purchase Orders

I can't seem to find any source that processes the f4311z or f4301z files.

Where can I find the program that actually processes and creates purchase orders from these files?

We are using World and One world, release levels world = A73
One world =
b7333 xe.

A: The F4301Z and F4311Z are indicated by JDE as OneWorld files. I'm not sure how they are used in OneWorld or in a coexistence environment.

There is not a batch PO creation program analogous to the batch sales order creation program (P40211Z).

The purchase order generator (P43011) allows you to generate purchase orders by selecting items that are below their reorder point, by either Supplier number or Buyer Number.

See option 14 on menu G43A13 for this program.

If you want to create PO's in a true batch fashion, similar to the way that the batch sales order creation program works, then you are going to have to write a new program.

The last conversion project that I worked on required that we convert the PO's from the old Wang system to JDE, and we wrote an RPG program that read data from a Wang flat file and created the F4301 & F4311 records.

Question 95: AS400 Fax

We presently use Create!Form to print custom forms (picks, bols, etc) to printer. We now want to fax those forms. We are evaluating the Create!Fax module and know it should work with Create!Form but just had a demo from Bizcom and was impressed with its simplicity.

If anyone is using any of these faxing solutions, can you give your evaluations/opinions?

A: I am not sure if you will be able to use another fax software vendor. Create!Form creates a postscript document that is sent to the printer. I am concerned that when using a different vendor, the postscript language would ultimately be sent, and not the actual document.

Conflicts usually arise when using two fax vendor programs.

Question 96: A/P Attachment

When we run our checks (P04572), you have the option to Save Spool File (on form P04257, Work with Payment Groups) so that after running checks, you still have the spool file. This works just fine but I recently noticed that the Check Attachment spool file (P04573 I think) does NOT go out on SAV after printing. There is not a DW form for Check Attachments so you can change any overrides either. We never noticed this until recently when our check attachments got "lost" and had nothing to reprint!

What am I missing here?

A: You need to do CHGPRTF S04573 and press F4, then F10. Page down 4 or 5 times and look for SAVE SPOOL FILE change to *YES and you will be a happy camper.
Do a "change printer" file, 'CHGPRTF' on the command line and prompt it with F4. Type in S04573 and hit enter. Hit F10 for additional parameters and scroll down about 7 pages and put *yes on the 'Save spool file' option.

Question 97: External Sales Process

We are investigating an e-commerce web site and need a way to feed orders into JD Edwards from the web site. It should be "almost real time". The web interface will be hosted on the AS400. I am looking for a method that will provide a clean interface that will not be too involved to setup. If anyone has had experience with this could you tell me how you did it and what problems/benefits you have had.

Is there an external process provided by JDE for something like this? Is there a Z file batch update, edi?

A: There is an inbound sales order program for EDI - P47011. This also provides a holding place for error transactions and screens to fix them-
G47212.

EDI or more correctly System 47 is probably your best bet. Feed the data into the P47011 and P47012 (header and detail) and run (I think) P47010 to create Sales Orders. I've seen this used to create SO's by Sales Reps entering data into Lotus notes, flat files FTP'ed in, uploads via Client Access file transfer or similar, etc, etc, you name it. It is robust, easily set up, and works well. Problems are fairly easily identified from the error reports and are usually down to incorrect Item numbers or Item/Branch plant missing, address numbers incorrect, etc.

Another suggestion is to use the Batch Import process on JDE. Load the F4001Z (Order header), F4011Z (Order detail), and the F4006Z file (Address). Then run the P40211Z Dreamwriter to import the files and perform all of the background processing, etc. This program can be found from menu G4212 option 24. We have a job setup in our job scheduler to run this hourly.

This is how you batch orders into JD Edwards from another source. If your web interface will be on your JDE machine then simply write an RPG program to populate these files from your e-commerce program's data files.

Question 98: Security Template

Is there any sort of security template that exists for setting up user security within the world environment? For example, AP users would have access to these menus etc.

A: Are you aware of the menu masking function in World? This is what you would use. It's explained in one of their basic manuals, I think Tech Foundations. You can make it simple or very complex, as there are 5 separate fields that you may use, and you may use as few or as many of them as you want.

For example, if you want to allow only the A/P department to access the A/P menus, you do this through menu masking. If your company is large enough, you can also get into hierarchical menu and menu option access within the A/P department.

Question 99: Office Vision 400

Does anyone have or know of any new solutions that are reasonable in price to do documents that will interface with JDE? We need a new one since AS400 Office Vision is being phased out.

These are documents that come from the old legacy 36 system Dream Writer, and believe it or not we are just getting ready to move off the System 36 (5360) at long last. I know Domino is the most popular but surely it is not the only way to go.

What are the alternatives?
A: Domino is a Lotus Notes application. Since Lotus is now a part of IBM anyone using Office Vision is encouraged to use Lotus Notes.

Here are a few of the 'replacement applications' I have found:

WordSmart, by JDP Consulting
Document Integrator, by Seacrtest
Intelligent Text Processing, by AIA/ITP
Wordsmart and ITP use MS Word, Document Integrator is strictly AS/400 green screen world.

Question 100: P98COVER

I modified the AR as of Aging Report (P034201 & R034201) to include terms code and description. SAR 2496257 was found in KG regarding the workaround but I don't fully understand what they want me to do. Here is the exact wording:

"Recompile printer file so that when DPSFD for printer file can find $HEADNG and $DETAIL. Before compilation, only HEADNG & DETAIL w/o $ sign."

What does it mean?

A: They are referring to record format names. If you do a DSPFD (display file description) command on the existing printer file (R034201), at the bottom of that display/listing is a list of the record formats in the printer file. Record format names that start '$' or '@' are NOT defined in the printer file DDS source. They are generated when you go through the JDE report design aid. These inserted record format names deal with printing the cover pages. If not in there, you won't be able to print those.

It sounds like you are compiling things outside the SVR (we do all the time). You have to add the cover page information to the bottom of the DDS (R034201).

Index

www.ingramcontent.com/pod-product-compliance
Lightning Source LLC
La Vergne TN
LVHW052302060326
832902LV00021B/3678